Superpower Games

Superpower Games

*Applying Game Theory to
Superpower Conflict*

Steven J. Brams

Yale University Press
New Haven and London

Designed by James J. Johnson
and set in Times Roman type. Printed in the United States of
America by Murray Printing Co., Westford, Mass.

Library of Congress Cataloging in Publication Data

Brams, Steven J.
  Superpower games.

  Bibliography: p.
  Includes index.
    1. Military policy—Mathematical models.   2. United
States—Military relations—Soviet Union.   3. Soviet Union—
Military relations—United States.   4. International relations—
Mathematical models.   I. Title.
UA11.B66 1985   355′.0335′0151   84–21876
ISBN 0–300–03323–0 (alk. paper)
ISBN 0–300–03364–8 (pbk. : alk. paper)

*The paper in this book meets the guidelines for
permanence and durability of the Committee on
Production Guidelines for Book Longevity of the Council
on Library Resources.*

10 9 8 7 6 5 4 3 2 1

Wars begin with conscious and reasoned decisions based on the calculation, made by *both* parties, that they can achieve more by going to war than by remaining at peace.

—MICHAEL HOWARD,
The Causes of War and Other Essays (1983)

Nuclear weapons exist. The knowledge of how to make them exists and cannot be made to vanish.

—SOLLY ZUCKERMAN,
Nuclear Illusion and Reality (1982)

There is no guarantee that strategic studies can or will make a difference [between wise and foolish policy decisions], but that possibility is sufficient justification for the enterprise.

—COLIN S. GRAY,
Strategic Studies and Public Policy (1982)

Contents

Figures and Tables

Preface

There is considerable confusion about the logic—or illogic—that fuels superpower conflict. In this book, I attempt to show how game theory can help elucidate the rational basis of different aspects of this baffling and deeply troubling conflict and suggest measures that might arrest its possibly ghastly consequences.

The *apparent* irrationality of such conflict stems, I believe, more from the intractable choices that players face in "superpower games" than from actions the players take that may, on occasion, appear irrational. Callous these leaders may be, but stupid they generally are not.

This is a controversial thesis, for it implies that we cannot generally blame our present difficulties on the unrestrained recklessness, gross negligence, or simple craziness of unenlightened leaders. By and large, I contend, these leaders act intelligently and prudently to advance their interests. However, because the games they find themselves embroiled in make conciliatory choices extremely problematic, their play frequently leads to pernicious conflict.

Games, play, and other game-theoretic terminology I shall use all have precise meanings in the mathematical theory of games. This usage differs sharply from the frivolity and playfulness we normally associate with games (how could something be serious if "it's only a game"?). In fact, games in game theory—whether serious or frivolous—are situations of interdependent decision making in which outcomes depend on the choices *all* players make. (Incidentally, I shall use the masculine pronoun form to refer to players throughout this book, but this usage is for convenience only and is not intended to suggest that strategizing is exclusively a male prerogative.)

I introduce new game-theoretic concepts (see Glossary for a compilation of the more technical terms in the book), and try to demonstrate their applicability to different Soviet-American conflicts in every chapter except the last. I assume a background in high school mathematics, but not specifically in game theory, which I develop from scratch. However, although my starting point is two-person noncooperative game theory, I make major emendations in the classical theory of von Neumann and Morgenstern* to render it pertinent to the study of superpower conflict. For example, dynamic models that explicate changes in this conflict over time, and probabilistic models that reflect its uncertainties, are particularly stressed.

I analyze various kinds of conflict in three different sets of games: (1) *deterrence games,* in which the side taking a provocative action that is immediately advantageous may precipitate eventual disaster for both players, presumably rendering the initial provocation irrational; (2) *arms-race games,* in which the rational choice of arming is unconditionally best but leads to an outcome worse for both players than disarming, which, however, is unstable; and (3) *verification games,* in which one side tries to hide the truth and the other to discover it, but the optimal strategy for doing either may involve actions that are sometimes random or arbitrary. All these games have paradoxical elements, which I shall analyze as rigorously as seems necessary to indicate the difficulties the players confront in acting rationally. In addition, case studies of two major crises that embroiled the superpowers in different parts of the world are used to illustrate how game-theoretic models can be applied to the analysis of historical material.

---

*John von Neumann and Oskar Morgenstern, *Theory of Games and Economic Behavior,* 3d ed. (Princeton, NJ: Princeton University Press, 1953). For a fine critical exposition of game theory and related topics, see R. Duncan Luce and Howard Raiffa, *Games and Decisions: Introduction and Critical Survey* (New York: Wiley, 1957). An up-to-date technical treatment can be found in Guillermo Owen, *Game Theory,* 2d ed. (New York: Academic Press, 1982); a lucid nontechnical treatment is given in Morton D. Davis, *Game Theory: A Nontechnical Introduction,* rev. ed. (New York: Basic, 1983). Applications of game theory to political science are described in Steven J. Brams, *Game Theory and Politics* (New York: Free Press, 1975).

Throughout this book I develop one or more models that seem to fit an empirical situation, or class of situations, and then offer either theoretical refinements or suggest applications to real-world conflicts between the superpowers. Although I use a number of descriptive aids in the many figures in this book in order to make the models as accessible as possible, I recognize that a detailed mathematical argument may appear quite opaque at the beginning and requires a good deal of perseverance to follow and finally master. My hope is that the payoff for this effort—to use a game-theoretic term—proves worthwhile in terms of the insight it provides to the different conflicts.

My purpose in offering a strategic analysis of superpower conflict is not solely explanatory. As important as deductive, rational-choice models are to scientific inquiry, I believe normative analysis is even more important in the case of conflict as frightening as that threatening to engulf the superpowers and the rest of the world today. It would be flagrantly irresponsible not to recognize that nuclear weapons are a harsh fact of life—obscene as their use might be, since it could end this life—and to ponder how best to render nugatory any conceivable advantage that could arise from their use.

Accordingly, I try to demonstrate how the theoretical-empirical analysis can point the way to possible rational solutions to some superpower games that, if they do not solve these conflicts outright, may ameliorate them or resolve certain dilemmas. Whether it be robust probabilistic threats in the case of deterrence, conditional cooperation with detection in the case of the arms race, or the inducement to truth telling in the case of verification, I believe progress can be made in each of these areas with careful and systematic modeling that is both rationally grounded and empirically testable.

In my opinion, the theoretical foundations on which strategic analysis is based must be built so that sound policy can be formulated. These foundations, I believe, must be constructed from a fundamental understanding of the rational nature of conflict, especially when that conflict is international and there is good reason to believe, because of the high stakes, that decisions are not capricious or perverse but well thought out and justified in terms of desired ends.

Failure to probe the foundations leads to an abundance of turgid rhetoric, hollow shibboleths, and superficial solutions. Unfortunately, none of the games I discuss has an easy solution. Yet, if some problems

Acknowledgments

I am grateful to Morton D. Davis, Marek P. Hessel, Philip D. Straffin, Jr., and Donald Wittman for permission to use material from jointly authored papers, or ideas from these papers, in this book. Specific citations are given in the text, though only some parts of chapters 2 and 3 have been previously published in substantially the same form as given here.

I am also grateful for the valuable comments of Raymond Dacey, Peter C. Fishburn, and Donald Wittman on chapter 4, and Frank C. Zagare on chapters 1 and 2, though I have not always followed their suggestions. I am especially indebted to D. Marc Kilgour for his detailed and trenchant technical comments on chapters 1 and 4; they not only saved me from errors but also considerably strengthened the game-theoretic arguments. For financial assistance that helped in the preparation of this book, I thank the C. V. Starr Center for Applied Economics at New York University, the Ford Foundation under Grant No. 845-0354 (with William J. Baumol and Dietrich Fischer), and the National Science Foundation under Grant No. SES84-08505.

Nancy Fernandez skillfully typed the manuscript, and I am pleased to acknowledge her help again. I would also like to thank Marian Neal Ash at Yale University Press for the strong support she gave to the book and Kate Schmit for her excellent editing of the manuscript.

My family, as usual, has been very supportive. Indeed, they now take the intrusion of book writing so much in stride that shifts in schedules are becoming routine. But there is nothing routine about my poignant subject, which deserves all the cogent analysis it can get.

1 Deterrence

1.1. Introduction

Deterrence is the cornerstone of the national-security policies of not only the superpowers but other nations as well. By threatening untoward action against an opponent who initiates conflict, even at great potential cost to oneself, one seeks to deter the opponent from committing aggression in the first place.

The controversy over the viability of deterrence has largely concerned the rationality of adhering to a policy that can lead to enormous destruction—perhaps even mutual annihilation—if the policy fails. Even the party attacked would seem foolhardy to bring upon itself a disastrous outcome if, by compromising or—heaven forbid!—capitulating, it could do better. By fighting (irrationally?) to the bitter end, the party attacked would seem to violate the very canons of rationality on which deterrence rests. On the other hand, by caving in, or indicating that it might, it would seem to invite attack.[1]

1. Deterrence without the threat of nuclear weapons is analyzed in John J. Mearsheimer, *Conventional Deterrence* (Ithaca, NY: Cornell University Press, 1983). Historical accounts of the development of nuclear strategy, portraits of the personalities involved in the strategic nuclear debate over the past forty years, and recommendations for changes in current policy can be found in several recent works (in addition to those cited later): Arthur Macy Cox, *Russian Roulette—The Superpower Game* (New York: Times Books, 1982); Fred Kaplan, *The Wizards of Armageddon* (New York: Simon and Schuster, 1983); Harold Brown, *Thinking about National Security: Defense and Foreign*

A number of different nuclear doctrines to support deterrence have been proposed, perhaps the most notable being MAD, or "mutual assured destruction." The inclusion of *mutual* in the MAD doctrine implies that each side can destroy the other, even if attacked first; this reciprocal vulnerability is presumed to make deterrence stable, at least as long as the mutual destruction is "assured."

Sometimes MAD is used to denote "mutual assured deterrence," with the means for assuring deterrence not necessarily assumed to be the destruction of society. Whereas "countervalue," which is stressed in the doctrine of mutual assured destruction, refers to the destruction of cities and industries, "counterforce" stresses the destruction of military forces, particularly missile sites, and command and control facilities. Zuckerman contends that "from the operational point of view there is practically no difference, apart from the verbal one, between what is now called counterforce and what is termed countervalue."[2] Other strategies, such as "damage-limitation" and "war-fighting" defenses after a limited nuclear attack—should deterrence fail—are also discussed in the national-international security literature.[3]

The rather arcane debate about deterrence and its alternatives is generally not about whether one should respond to attack, but how. In this chapter, by contrast, I shall focus on the rationality of uncertain responses. Wieseltier favors a sober kind of deterrence, coupled with disarmament; he argues that "deterrence . . . does not require certainty. Doubt is quite enough."[4] The question I seek to clarify in this chapter is what kind of doubt is best.

Policy in a Dangerous World (Boulder, CO: Westview, 1983); Bruce M. Russett, *The Prisoners of Insecurity* (San Francisco: Freeman, 1983); Harvard Nuclear Study Group, *Living with Nuclear Weapons* (New York: Bantam, 1983); Freeman Dyson, *Weapons and Hope* (New York: Harper and Row, 1984); Robert Jervis, *The Illogic of American Nuclear Strategy* (Ithaca, NY: Cornell University Press, 1984); Jonathan Schell, *The Abolition* (New York: Knopf, 1984); and Dietrich Fischer, *Preventing War in the Nuclear Age* (Totowa, NJ: Rowman and Allanheld, 1984).

2. Solly Zuckerman, *Nuclear Illusion and Reality* (New York: Viking, 1982). p. 53.

3. See, for example, Keith B. Payne, *Nuclear Deterrence in U.S.-Soviet Relations* (Boulder, CO: Westview, 1982); and William H. Baugh, *The Politics of Nuclear Balance: Ambiguity and Continuity in Strategic Policies* (New York: Longman, 1984), who offers an interesting classification of the "plethora of doctrines" along three dimensions (pp. 71–76).

4. Leon Wieseltier, *Nuclear War, Nuclear Peace* (New York: Holt, Rinehart and Winston, 1983), p. 61.

Bundy places such doubt in the category of "existential" deterrence: "The terrible and unavoidable uncertainties in any recourse to nuclear war create what could be called 'existential' deterrence, where the function of the adjective is to distinguish this phenomenon from anything based on strategic theories of declared policies or even international commitments."[5] I shall, by comparison, try to show in this chapter how even "terrible and unavoidable uncertainties" can be analyzed using game theory. These uncertainties presumably enhance what some have called "extended deterrence" (that is, deterrence that extends beyond the superpowers), which has deterred war in Europe though not in other regions (for example, the Middle East and Southeast Asia) where the superpowers have a stake but their interests are much less well defined than in the core regions ("spheres of influence") of which they are members. The fluid situations in more peripheral regions have, curiously, led to some of the bloodiest and most dangerous conflicts in the East-West struggle both to hold the allegiance of allies and contain the other side's influence.

Finally, there is the question of the proper mix of nuclear and nonnuclear forces, based on the doctrines of "graduated deterrence" or "flexible response" that are meant to make one's deterrent more credible. This question is particularly germane to deterrence in Western Europe, where the issue of the use of tactical and strategic nuclear weapons to deter a Soviet attack is hotly debated. I shall touch upon this issue in section 1.7 in a discussion of the doctrine of "no first use" and in section 10 on the use of "certain equivalents" of probabilistic (nuclear) threats. In addition, the case studies in chapter 2 provide a theoretical explication and empirical examples of how an artful combination of conventional means and nuclear threats were used in tandem to prevent nuclear escalation.

Apart from the question of what specific doctrines best ensure deterrence, can deterrence as a general policy be justified? Brams and Hessel suggested that one possible resolution of the apparently conflicting conceptions of rationality embodied in deterrence is that carrying out a threat when deterrence fails, though irrational in the single play of a game, may well be rational in repeated play.[6] The reason is that a

5. McGeorge Bundy, "The Bishops and the Bomb," *New York Review of Books*, June 16, 1983, p. 4.

6. Steven J. Brams and Marek P. Hessel, "Threat Power in Sequential Games," *International Studies Quarterly* 28, no. 1 (March 1984):15–36.

carried-out threat enhances one's credibility—in doing the apparently irrational thing in a single play—so that, over the long run, one can develop a sufficiently fearsome reputation to deter future opponents. Thereby, although losing on occasion in the short run, one can gain over time.

Zagare offered another game-theoretic resolution.[7] Positing several conditions that the logic of deterrence requires in a game, he showed that, taken together, they single out the well-known game, Prisoners' Dilemma. His "crucial" requirement—credibility—distinguishes another well-known game, Chicken, from Prisoners' Dilemma; without this requirement, he argued, the player being deterred would not believe a threat would be carried out if it took the prohibited action.

I shall discuss these different resolutions by comparing Prisoners' Dilemma and Chicken in section 1.2 (and later in section 1.8, after the development of the deterrence model), focusing on the short-term (single-play) versus long-term (repeated-play) points of view about deterrence that each resolution, respectively, purports to capture. Then I shall argue that the largely uncharted territory between single and repeated play of a deterrence game can be better understood by making explicit the likely expected-payoff calculations of the players.

Toward this end, I shall introduce Ellsberg's notion of "critical risk" and demonstrate how it can be derived as a consequence of players' optimal choices in the sequential game to be used to model deterrence.[8] Next, developing implications of Schelling's concept of a probabilistic threat, which is not carried out with certainty but instead "leaves something to chance,"[9] I shall show how the idea of mixed strategies in two-person zero-sum games (to be defined later) can be extended to two-person nonzero-sum games like Prisoners' Dilemma and Chicken, wherein both players can benefit from threatening each other.

7. Frank C. Zagare, "Toward a Reconciliation of Game Theory and the Theory of Mutual Deterrence" (Department of Political Science, Boston University, 1983, mimeographed).

8. Daniel Ellsberg, "The Theory and Practice of Blackmail," in *Bargaining: Formal Theories of Negotiation*, ed. Oran R. Young (Urbana, IL: University of Illinois Press, 1975), pp. 343–63.

9. Thomas C. Schelling, *The Strategy of Conflict* (Cambridge, MA: Harvard University Press, 1960).

I begin with the analysis of simple 2 × 2 games in normal, or matrix, form, in which two players each can choose two strategies. The analysis is then extended to 2 × 4 games, in which one player moves first and the other responds, giving the second player four strategies. The latter games highlight the problem that preemption by the first-moving player may create in a deterrence situation and, in addition, help to identify the game (Chicken) that seems best suited to model deterrence.

But even the 2 × 4 extension of Chicken is too simple. Accordingly, a more complex game in extensive form, based on a game-tree representation of Chicken that also incorporates formal calculations of risk, is proposed, which in turn is recast in normal form.

Optimal probabilistic threats of the players are derived under a variety of different assumptions, including the possibility that deterrence may fail, that one side adopts a policy of "no first use," and that the "incredibility" of threats may diminish their deterrent value. The trade-off between effective and credible threats, which I define precisely later, may make achieving both impossible.

I suggest that, in a world of uncertainty, probabilistic threats may be superior to deterministic threats (which are carried out with certainty)— and the concomitant policy of MAD should deterrence fail. In particular, threats that have a certain kind of "robustness" are analyzed in light of their ability to achieve stable deterrence and prevent an escalation of conflict between the superpowers that could lead to nuclear war.

I share Morgan's view (and those of others extolling uncertainty quoted earlier) that "on balance, deterrence is not usually a matter of evoking certainty of retaliatory response so much as evoking a beneficial uncertainty."[10] Surely the quantitative issue is what level of

---

10. Patrick M. Morgan, *Deterrence: A Conceptual Analysis*, 2d ed. (Beverly Hills, CA: Sage, 1983), p. 119. A more paradoxical conception of deterrence is suggested by Jack Hirshleifer, "The Economic Approach to Conflict" (Department of Economics, University of California, Los Angeles, 1984), p. 20: "If he [a player] can reliably threaten to do what he does not want to do, he won't have to do it!" This suggests a player acts rationally if he makes an irrevocable commitment to do something irrational (that is, carry out his threat of retaliation), for, as Krauthammer puts it, nuclear weapons "are built in order never to be used." Charles Krauthammer, "On Nuclear Morality," in *Nuclear Arms: Ethics, Strategy, Politics*, ed. R. James Woolsey (San Francisco: Institute for Contemporary Studies, 1984), p. 13. I shall try to show later how probabilistic threats can help resolve this apparent paradox—that the *possibility* of using nuclear weapons (by

uncertainty is "beneficial"; a primary goal of this chapter is to render explicit a compelling basis for making this calculation.

I conclude that probabilistic threats, perhaps unwittingly, are in fact implicit in policies and procedures used by the superpowers today, including even the destruction—of cities or military forces—that each side promises to visit on the other (with certainty) should deterrence fail. One task of a rational theory of deterrence, I believe, is to demonstrate that certainty is an illusion: an ineradicable uncertainty is inherent in the deterministic threats that are promulgated by the superpowers. The intellectual challenge that such a theory faces is to justify such policies and procedures and show how they might be improved upon, in a manner consistent with the theory.

1.2. Prisoners' Dilemma versus Chicken

The 2×2 games of Prisoners' Dilemma and Chicken, in which two players can rank the four outcomes from best to worst, are illustrated in figure 1.1. Because the players do not order any two outcomes the same—that is, there are no ties between ranks—these are *strictly* ordinal games. In the later analysis, I shall assume that the players can assign numerical values, or cardinal utilities, to the outcomes.

The players in each game are assumed to be able to choose between the strategies of cooperation (c) and noncooperation (c̄). The choices of strategies by each player lead to four possible outcomes, ranked by the players from best (4) to worst (1). The first number in the ordered pair that defines each outcome is assumed to be the ranking of the row player, the second number the ranking of the column player. Thus, the outcome (3,3) in both games is considered to be next best for both players, but no presumption is made about whether this outcome is closer to each player's best (4) or next-worst (2) outcome.

The short-hand verbal descriptions given in figure 1.1 for each outcome are intended to convey the qualitative nature of the outcomes, based on the players' rankings, in each game. Both of these games are *symmetric:* the two players rank the outcomes along the main diagonal the same, whereas the ranks of the off-diagonal outcomes are mirror

---

retaliating with some probability less than one) can more credibly imply their nonuse than *certain* retaliation.

FIGURE 1.1   Prisoners' Dilemma and Chicken

Prisoners' Dilemma

           Column

	c	c̄
Row c	(3,3) Compromise	(1,4) Column advantaged
c̄	(4,1) Row advantaged	(2,2) Conflict

(2,2) ← Dominant strategy for row

↑ Dominant strategy for column

Chicken

           Column

	c	c̄
Row c	(3,3) Compromise	(2,4) Column wins
c̄	(4,2) Row wins	(1,1) Disaster

Key: (x,y) = (rank of row, rank of column)
4 = best; 3 = next best; 2 = next worst; 1 = worst
c = cooperation; c̄ = noncooperation
Circled outcomes are Nash equilibria

images of each other. (In sections 2.2 and 3.2 I briefly recount the stories that give each game its name.) Because of the symmetry of the games, each of the two players faces the same problems of strategic choice.

In both games, each player obtains his next-best outcome by choosing c (compromise), if the other players also does, but both have an incentive to defect from this outcome to obtain their best outcomes of 4 by choosing c̄ when the other player chooses c. Yet, if both choose c̄, they bring upon themselves their next-worst outcome ("conflict") in Prisoners' Dilemma, their worst outcome ("disaster") in Chicken.

These games are nonconstant-sum, because both players can do simultaneously better at some outcomes (for example, cc) than others (c̄c̄). Since what one player "wins" the other does not necessarily "lose," the sum of payoffs (or ranks) at every outcome is not constant; the games are therefore called *variable-sum.* They are also *games of partial conflict*—as opposed to (constant-sum) *games of total conflict,* in which the benefits that redound to one player invariably hurt the other.

The dilemma in Prisoners' Dilemma is that both players have a *dominant strategy* of choosing c̄: whatever the other player chooses (c or c̄), c is better; but the choice of c̄ by both leads to (2,2), which is *Pareto-inferior,* or worse for both players, than (3,3). In addition, (2,2) is a *Nash equilibrium* (that is, neither player has an incentive to deviate unilaterally from this outcome because he would do worse if he did), whereas (3,3) is not stable in this sense.[11]

Presumably, rational players would each choose their dominant, or unconditionally best, strategies of c̄, resulting in the Pareto-inferior (2,2) Nash equilibrium; because of its stability, and despite (3,3)'s being a better outcome for both, neither player would be motivated to depart from (2,2). Should (3,3) somehow manage to be chosen, however, both players would be tempted to depart from it to try to do still better, rendering it unstable. Put another way, mutual cooperation would seem hard to sustain because each player would have an incentive to double-cross his opponent.

---

11. John Nash, "Non-cooperative Games," *Annals of Mathematics* 54 (1951):286–95. I consider here equilibria only in *pure strategies,* which involve choosing single (nonprobabilistic) courses of action; in section 2.6 I shall contrast these equilibria with "nonmyopic equilibria."

In Chicken there are two Nash equilibria in pure strategies, (4,2) and (2,4), both of which are *Pareto-superior* since there are no other outcomes better for *both* players. But each player, in choosing his strategy c̄ associated with the Nash equilibrium favorable to himself [(4,2) for row, (2,4) for column], risks the disastrous (1,1) outcome (should the other player also choose c̄).

The fact that neither player has a dominant strategy in Chicken means that each's better strategy choice (c or c̄) depends on the strategy choice of the other player. This interdependence gives each player an incentive to *threaten* to choose c̄, hoping the other will concede by choosing c so that the threatener can obtain his preferred Nash equilibrium. As in Prisoners' Dilemma, the compromise (3,3) outcome is unappealing because, should it be chosen, it is not stable.

It is hard to say which game poses more obdurate problems for the players. As a model of the superpower arms race (see chapter 3), Prisoners' Dilemma has been used to explain why the United States and the Soviet Union have failed to reach agreement on major arms-control measures and continue to suffer the burdens of tremendous arms expenditures, which both could benefit from reducing. As a model of confrontation situations like the Cuban missile crisis (see chapter 2), Chicken has been used to explain why the superpowers have been willing to flirt with nuclear war on occasion.

Ostensibly, Chicken would seem closer to the intimidation implicit in a deterrence game in which the United States and the Soviet Union threaten each other with MAD. However, Zagare argues that, under a policy of MAD, a threatener would be unwilling to carry out the "incredible" threat that brings the players to (1,1) in Chicken—at least of the nuclear variety.[12] Thus, he maintains, in order for one's threat to be credible, it must be the case that 2 and 1 in Chicken are interchanged so that when a player chooses c̄ he will know that the deterrent threat of the other player—to respond by choosing c̄ himself—is rational to carry out. It is rational in Prisoner's Dilemma, which in fact reverses 2 and 1 in Chicken, but not in Chicken, wherein the choice of c̄ by one player would seem to call for the choice of c by the other.

Indeed, if deterrence is viewed as a 2 × 4 version of Chicken, in

12. Zagare, "Toward a Reconciliation of Game Theory and the Theory of Mutual Deterrence."

which one player (row) chooses first and the other (column) responds to his strategy choice—giving column four possible strategies, as shown in figure 1.2—then column's choice of "tat-for-tit" (choose c̄ if row chooses c; choose c if row choses c̄) is dominant. But then row, who does not have a dominant strategy himself but can anticipate column's choice of tat-for-tit in a *game of complete information* (that is, one in which the players have full information about the rules of play—order of choice, payoffs of all players, and so on), should choose c̄ to ensure

FIGURE 1.2   2 × 4 Versions of Prisoners' Dilemma and Chicken

Prisoners' Dilemma

		Column			
		c regardless c/c	c̄ regardless c̄/c̄	Tit-for-tat c/c̄	Tat-for-tit c̄/c
Row	c	(3,3)	(1,4)	(3,3)	(1,4)
	c̄	(4,1)	(2,2)	(2,2)	(4,1)

↑
Dominant strategy
for column

Chicken

		Column			
		c regardless c/c	c̄ regardless c̄/c̄	Tit-for-tat c/c̄	Tat-for-tit c̄/c
Row	c	(3,3)	(2,4)	(3,3)	(2,4)
	c̄	(4,2)	(1,1)	(1,1)	(4,2)

↑
Dominant strategy
for column

Key: (x,y) = (rank of row, rank of column)
   A/B = choose A if row chooses first strategy/choose B if row chooses second strategy
   4 = best; 3 = next best; 2 = next worst; 1 = worst
   c = cooperation; c̄ = noncooperation
   Circled outcomes are Nash equilibria

(4,2), which is a Nash equilibrium, rather than c, which would yield (2,4). There are other Nash equilibria in this game, as shown in figure 1.2, but (4,2) is the only one associated with column's dominant strategy. Unfortunately for column, it induces his next-worst outcome, which I have elsewhere called the "paradox of inducement."[13]

This analysis would seem to establish that a threatener (for example, column in figure 1.2), in responding to a provocation brought on by the threatenee's (row's) choice of c̄ in Chicken, should not himself choose a strategy that results in (1,1). The reason is that it would be irrational for column to bring on himself (1,1) rather than (4,2) in this game.

With 2 and 1 interchanged in Chicken as shown in figure 1.2, however, c̄/c̄ is dominant for column in the resulting 2 × 4 version of Prisoners' Dilemma (also shown in figure 1.2). Anticipating this choice, row will chose c̄, too, thereby rendering the Pareto-inferior Nash equilibrium rational in this version of Prisoners' Dilemma, as well as the version in figure 1.1.

But note that c̄/c̄ is a strategy of unconditional noncooperation *not* dependent on row's prior strategy choice. It therefore seems *not* what is usually meant by a threat strategy ("I'll cooperate if you will; otherwise I won't"), in which there is a reward for good behavior and a penalty for bad behavior. Also, the (2,2) outcome in Prisoners' Dilemma does not seem very descriptive of "mutual assured destruction" that (1,1) in (nuclear) Chicken connotes.

Contrary to Zagare,[14] therefore, Prisoners' Dilemma would not seem *the* prototypical deterrence game. But how, then, can one explain the apparently irrational choice of (1,1) in Chicken? If this choice cannot be rationally justified, deterrence makes little strategic sense, given that a policy of MAD has some nonzero probability of failing and someday, as a consequence, the two superpowers will eventually be called upon to do the incredible.

To circumvent what might be called the "rationality crisis" of deterrence, Brams and Hessel proposed a model that assumes repeated plays of a game, arguing that "if plays are repeated, there is nothing

13. Steven J. Brams, *Paradoxes in Politics: An Introduction to the Nonobvious in Political Science* (New York: Free Press, 1976), chap. 5.
14. Zagare, "Toward a Reconciliation of Game Theory and the Theory of Mutual Deterrence."

irrational about suffering a (temporary) loss if the long-run gain from deterring future opponents more than offsets this loss."[15] This long-run gain might be expressed by the (2,2) outcome in Prisoners' Dilemma, which would, in effect, be a *supergame,* or a game that comprises repeated plays of a component game. It would sum the value of cooperative play of Chicken in "many" instances (when deterrence succeeded) and its noncooperative play in a "few" instances (when deterrence failed).

In attempting to justify the rationality of deterrence, Brams and Hessel contend that "Zagare's analysis takes account of the long-run gain without revealing why a short-term loss may be necessary to achieve it."[16] At the same time, however, they admit that

if the short-term losses for both players incurred at (1,1) are devastating (e.g., nuclear war), the assumption of repeated play makes little sense. On the other hand, the *threat* of nuclear war, as in the Cuban missile crisis of October 1962, can and has been repeated, though we are by no means recommending nuclear brinkmanship as a policy but simply trying to explain its continued use.[17]

The explanation of both Zagare and Brams and Hessel is based on an analysis of simple ordinal games that do not admit the explicit calculation of expected utilities (or payoffs) that would accrue to players—willing, on occasion, to carry out threats—for maintaining their credibility in order to deter opponents. To provide a more sophisticated explanation of the rationality crisis, and how it might be resolved, what is needed, I believe, is a model that allows one to balance two considerations: (1) the "effectiveness" of a threat (measured by the cost it

---

15. Brams and Hessel, "Threat Power in Sequential Games," p. 34 n. 6.

16. Brams and Hessel, "Threat Power in Sequential Games," p. 34 n. 6. Of course, a player may find it expedient to misrepresent his preferences if information about them is incomplete (for example, try to make it appear that his preferences are those of Prisoners' Dilemma and not Chicken), which is a form of deception that will be discussed in section 2.3.

17. Brams and Hessel, "Threat Power in Sequential Games," p. 34 n. 6; italics in original. Gauthier also questions the value of the "long run" in a nuclear exchange: "For the US to claim that, despite its preference for minimizing nuclear devastation, retaliation would be advantageous in the long run because it would make the future use of a retaliatory policy credible and so effective would be to overlook the probable lack of a long run." David Gauthier, "Deterrence, Maximization, and Rationality," *Ethics* 94, no. 3 (April 1984):479.

inflicts on a threatenee if carried out) and (2) the "incredibility" of the threat (measured by its cost to the threatener in carrying it out).

1.3. The Trade-off between the Effectiveness and Credibility of a Threat

Ideally, to deter an opponent, a threat should be both effective and credible. Its effectiveness increases the more damage it causes the player who ignores it; its credibility increases the lower its cost to the threatener to carry it out.

Unfortunately, the ideal for the player who seeks to deter his opponent is not readily attainable. Normally, there is a trade-off between effectiveness and credibility: as effectiveness increases, credibility declines, because the respective costs to each player of a carried-out threat tend to increase simultaneously. Thus, threatening nuclear war may be effective—if carried out, it will inflict enormous costs—but quite incredible because it may be equally damaging to the threatener to carry out his threat if the threatenee will respond in kind. As McNamara recently put it, "One cannot build a credible threat on an incredible action."[18]

There have been a number of practical solutions proposed to this problem, including the doctrines of "graduated deterrence" and "flexible response," both somewhat akin to a "tit-for-tat" policy, with the force threatened in response to an attack roughly proportional to the provocation. This kind of policy poses a deterministic threat; probabilistic threats that create "strategic uncertainty" have also been proposed,[19] though, with one noteworthy exception,[20] not formalized or rigorously analyzed in variable-sum games like Chicken.

These latter kinds of threats might take the following form: "If you cooperate, so will I (with certainty); but if you do not, my response—

18. Robert S. McNamara, "Inviting War," *New York Times*, September 9, 1983, p. A27.

19. Donald M. Snow, *The Nuclear Future: Toward a Strategy of Uncertainty* (University, AL: University of Alabama Press, 1983).

20. Schelling, *Strategy of Conflict*, chap. 7. In fact, Schelling's notion of probabilistic threats (and promises), which he argues make large and otherwise indivisible threats "divisible," is virtually identical to that developed here. What Schelling does not do is formalize the trade-off between effectiveness and credibility, which I shall do in this section and then develop some of its implications.

without saying what it is—will be appropriate,'' which has sometimes been referred to as ''calculated ambiguity.'' If there are only two possible responses to a provocative act—to ignore it or retaliate—then this statement suggests a good deal of uncertainty about whether the threatener will retaliate.

To illustrate the nature of, and calculations that may underlie, a probabilistic threat, consider the symbolic representation of Chicken in figure 1.3, where (r_i, c_j) represents the payoffs to the row (r_i) and column (c_j) players, respectively. These payoffs are assumed to be cardinal utilities, where a_4 and b_4 are the best payoffs, a_1 and b_1 the worst. Thus, the subscripts correspond to the ranks in figure 1.1.

Assume column is the threatener. Then the first part of his threat, ''If you cooperate, so will I (with certainty),'' implies that if row chooses c, column will also choose c, leading to (r_3, c_3), each player's next-best payoff. The second part of column's threat, ''if you do not, my response . . . will be appropriate,'' suggests a *mixed strategy* on column's part: if row chooses c̄, column will choose c with some probability p, c̄ with complementary probability $1 - p$.[21] By contrast, since a pure strategy is one in which c or c̄ would be chosen with certainty ($p = 1$ or 0), it is simply a special case of a mixed strategy.

Presumably, column's threat will deter row from choosing c̄ if

$$r_3 > r_4 p + r_1(1 - p), \tag{1.1}$$

that is, if column chooses a p such that row's payoff from cooperation is greater than his expected payoff from noncooperation. Without loss of generality, the right-hand side of inequality (1.1) can be simplified by assuming that row's highest payoff is $r_4 = 1$, his lowest payoff is $r_1 = 0$, and $0 < r_2 < r_3 < 1$.

Given this normalization of payoffs, if $r_3 > p$ (or $p < r_3$), it will be in row's interest to choose c. For if row chooses c̄, the risk that column will respond by choosing c̄ himself (with probability $1 - p$) will lower row's expected payoff below r_3, which is the payoff he can ensure when he chooses c and column responds with c.

21. Henceforth, I shall assume that the rules of the game allow players to make threats—probabilistic or deterministic—and take measures to ensure that they will be carried out. The credibility problems that precommitting oneself to a threat poses in theory, and how such precommitments are made believable in practice, will be discussed in this and future sections.

FIGURE 1.3   Symbolic Representation
of Chicken

Column

		C	Ĉ
Row	C	(r_3, c_3)	$\boxed{(r_2, c_4)}$
	Ĉ	$\boxed{(r_4, c_2)}$	(r_1, c_1)

Key: (r_i, c_j) = (payoff to row, payoff to column)
r_4, c_4 = best payoffs; r_3, c_3 = next-best payoffs; r_2, c_2 = next-worst payoffs; r_1, c_1 = worst payoffs
C = cooperation; Ĉ = noncooperation
Circled outcomes are Nash equilibria

The p that satisfies (1.1) when it is an *equality*, and makes row indifferent between choosing C and Ĉ, is what Ellsberg calls the "critical risk."[22] Ellsberg interprets it in terms of row's assessment of column's resolve to carry out his threat: if row thinks that, when he chooses Ĉ, column will respond with Ĉ with probability $1 - p$, given by inequality (1.1) that implies $p < r_3$ (with normalized payoffs), it is better for row to cooperate in the first place.

Define the *effectiveness* of column's threat to row, *Eff*(C), to be the difference between row's payoff from cooperation (r_3) and the expected damage row will suffer if he chooses not to cooperate $[r_4 p + r_1(1 - p)]$:

$$Eff(\text{C}) = r_3 - [r_4 p + r_1(1 - p)].$$

Define the *incredibility* of column's threat to row, *Inc*(C), to be the difference between column's payoff if row cooperates (c_3) and the expected damage column will suffer if row does not cooperate $[c_2 p + c_1(1 - p)]$:

$$Inc(\text{C}) = c_3 - [c_2 p + c_1(1 - p)].$$

22. Ellsberg, "Theory and Practice of Blackmail."

If, as before, each player's highest and lowest payoffs are assumed to be 1 and 0, respectively, in normalized form

$$Eff(c) = r_3 - p;$$

$$Inc(c) = c_3 - c_2 p.$$

Clearly, when $p = 0$ (or $1 - p = 1$, that is, the threat will be carried out with certainty), $Eff(c) = r_3$ and $Inc(c) = c_3$, their maximum values. Hence, the most effective threat in Chicken is the most incredible, which is, of course, the portentous irony that a threatener, who necessarily suffers in carrying out his threat, must contemplate.

But, in comparative terms (the legitimacy of such comparisons will be discussed shortly), it would appear that the threatener suffers less than the threatenee in Chicken once the threatenee has chosen $\bar{c}$. After all, if row chooses $\bar{c}$, column faces the choice between staying at his next-worst outcome (c_2) or further escalating the conflict—after row has chosen $\bar{c}$—to his worst (c_1). This move by column, on the other hand, means row's payoff in Chicken changes from r_4 to r_1. If one assumes that the worst outcome for both players is equally bad (for example, nuclear war), then it would appear—insofar as interpersonal comparisons of utilities can be made—that row, in going from r_4 to r_1, would be made worse off than column in going from c_2 to c_1.

Are such comparisons defensible? If so, what is the proper basis for such a comparison? Consider the first question. *Any* comparison of two players' payoffs, or trade-offs that involve these, can be challenged as irrelevant. In game theory, the payoffs of a player at an outcome are assumed to embody *all* that he values, including his feelings—altruistic, vengeful, or whatever—about other players at this outcome. Therefore, his rational calculations should reflect only his own payoffs.

If this is the case, then any trade-off that decreases the effectiveness of a threat (as measured by the harm it causes the threatenee) to increase its credibility (as measured by the harm it causes the threatener) is beside the point. The inescapable fact is that carrying out a threat is going to hurt the threatener, *given that his payoff is his sole concern.* Thereby the rationality of retaliating, even on a probabilistic basis, is cast in doubt, which Freedman, in his historical treatment, argues is the crux of the ongoing debate about what response is appropriate should deterrence fail.[23]

This problem ties into the second question—what should be compared? The concepts of effectiveness and incredibility defined earlier presumed the basis of comparison to be the cooperative outcome, (r_3,c_3), versus an expected value if one player did not cooperate, whereas previously I assumed (in the deterministic case) the basis to be the outcome (r_4,c_2) versus (r_1,c_1) if row did not cooperate.

Clearly, the first view is proper if the players start from the cooperative outcome, (r_3,c_3). But if, say, row defies column's threat and moves to (r_4,c_2), the players are in a different position, and column may feel it appropriate to reassess his probabilistic threat.

If he carries out this threat, both players suffer, and this is the agonizing dilemma for column at this point. Zagare would argue that there is no real dilemma, at least if the deterrence game is Prisoners' Dilemma, not Chicken; accordingly, once row chooses $\bar{c}$, it is rational for column to respond with $\bar{c}$ because, in Prisoners' Dilemma, the $\bar{c}\bar{c}$ outcome is better for column than the $\bar{c}c$ outcome.[24]

Unlike Prisoners' Dilemma, in which players never have an incentive to make their threats probabilistic, in Chicken they do, for a deterministic response of $\bar{c}$ by the threatener to the threatenee's choice of $\bar{c}$ would appear quite incredible. To be sure, in repeated play of Chicken there may be justification for incurring costs now to deter future aggressors, as suggested in section 1.2. But in a one-shot game, a probabilistic threat, if less effective, is more credible and would, at least, create doubt in the threatenee's mind about the advisability of choosing $\bar{c}$ in the first place.

Recall that the critical-risk calculation offers quantitative guidance on the optimal probability to incorporate in a probabilistic threat. However, it presumes that column knows row's payoffs and can, armed with this information, choose a p, according to inequality (1.1), that will make it unprofitable for row to risk choosing $\bar{c}$.

Yet, if the game is not one of complete information, column cannot

23. Lawrence Freedman, *The Evolution of Nuclear Strategy* (New York: St. Martin's, 1981), pp. 372–75.

24. Zagare, "Toward a Reconciliation of Game Theory and the Theory of Mutual Deterrence."

be sure that the p he chooses—or leads row to believe he will act upon—is low enough (that is, the probability of retaliation, $1 - p$, is high enough) that row will indeed be deterred. Moreover, since carrying out a threat, even on a probabilistic basis, will be costly to column, row may feel—with some justification—that this "incredibility cost" will, in the end, prevent column, once the process reaches (r_4, c_2), from carrying through on his threat to move to (r_1, c_1).

I believe there is a way out of this dilemma that does not entail interpersonal comparisons of utility or even require complete information about an opponent's payoffs. It does, however, require that the deterrence game be redefined in such a way as to take account of players' precommitments to threats and that there be procedures that ensure that they will be enforced. Before spelling out players' calculations in such a game and conditions for deterrence to be successful, I shall consider whether there are other games that may serve as the basis of a model of deterrence.

I argued in section 1.2 that the essence of a threat is a conditional statement, but column's dominant strategy of $\bar{c}/\bar{c}$ in the 2 × 4 version of Prisoners' Dilemma in figure 1.2 is unconditional; moreover, outcome (2,2) in Prisoners' Dilemma does not seem to characterize the horrendous consequences of nuclear war, should deterrence fail, which seems better characterized by outcome (1,1) in Chicken. Finally, earlier in this section I pointed out that once the threatenee chooses $\bar{c}$ in Prisoners' Dilemma, it is rational for the threatener to retaliate, which defines away what I believe to be the core issue of deterrence—whether the threatener should escalate, in response to the threatenee's choice of $\bar{c}$, by carrying out his threat and choosing $\bar{c}$ himself *when the rationality of this choice is suspect*.

This issue is raised starkly in Chicken, as I have just shown. Are there still other games in which this issue is also raised? There may indeed be, if the roles of the players are asymmetric (their rankings of outcomes are not the same along the main diagonal and mirror images of each other off the diagonal). However, if

1. the underlying game is symmetric,[25]

25. The validity of this symmetry assumption in the context of Soviet-American conflict is supported by the following statement of an authority on Soviet defense policy: "The answers [to the problems posed by nuclear war and nuclear weapons] the Soviet

2. the cooperative outcome (CC) is better for both players than the noncooperative outcome (c̄c̄), and

3. row prefers c̄c to CC to Cc̄, and column prefers Cc̄ to CC to c̄c,

only Chicken and Prisoners' Dilemma, among the 78 distinct 2×2 strictly ordinal games, meet all three criteria.[26]

Since Chicken, not Prisoners' Dilemma, seems better to capture both the threats implicit in a concept of deterrence and the difficulty of making them credible, I shall henceforth assume this to be the underlying game in the deterrence model—though, in section 1.8, after the development of this model, I shall reassess the validity of my position. What has so far been developed from the viewpoint of one player will now be developed from the viewpoint of both players in a full-fledged game-theoretic model in which time-dependent aspects of the deterrence game will be set forth unambiguously.

1.4. The Deterrence Game in Extensive Form

Although Chicken describes the payoffs the players derive from their pure (that is, single) strategy choices of c and c̄, it does not fully describe the rules of the deterrence game, including the sequence of play. For this purpose, it is necessary to give the game in *extensive form,* or *game tree,* that depicts the choices and (expected) payoffs of the players at each node, or choice point.

---

leaders have arrived at are not very different from those given by Western governments. . . . The Soviet Union has not been able to escape from the threat of nuclear annihilation. Its leaders and its people share our predicament.'' David Holloway, *The Soviet Union and the Arms Race* (New Haven: Yale University Press, 1983), p. 182.

26. For complete listings, see Anatol Rapoport and Melvin Guyer, ''A Taxonomy of 2×2 Games,'' *General Systems: Yearbook of the Society for General Systems Research* 11 (1965):203–14; and Steven J. Brams, ''Deception in 2×2 Games,'' *Journal of Peace Science* 2 (Spring 1977):171–203. For a partial listing that excludes the 21 games with a mutually best outcome, see Steven J. Brams, *Superior Beings: If They Exist, How Would We Know? Game-Theoretic Implications of Omniscience, Omnipotence, Immortality, and Incomprehensibility* (New York: Springer-Verlag, 1983), pp. 173–77. The 78 2×2 games, in which each player can strictly rank the four outcomes from best to worst, are structurally distinct in the sense that no interchange of rows, columns, or players can transform one of these games into any other.

From row's vantage point, he may choose either c or c̄, as shown at the top of the game tree in figure 1.4. Once he has made his choice, column may choose either c or c̄. The expected payoffs for row after he has made his choice (indicated by E_R), and the payoffs/expected payoffs for column after he has made his subsequent choice (indicated by E_C), are shown under their respective branches.[27]

Previously I defined p to be the probability that column would choose c in response to row's prior choice of c̄. Actually, this is a *conditional probability*, dependent on row's having chosen c̄. In fact, all three probabilities shown in figure 1.4 are assumed to be conditional on prior events, which can be defined as follows:

p = probability that column chooses c, given row's prior choice of c̄ (at bottom right);

q = probability that row chooses c, given column's prior choice of c̄ (right branch at bottom left);

s = probability that column chooses c, given row's prior choice of c (at bottom left).

Complementary conditional probabilities of choosing c̄ in each case—$1 - p$, $1 - q$, and $1 - s$—are also shown in figure 1.4.

The first two conditional probabilities, $1 - p$ and $1 - q$, define the probabilistic threats that I assume column and row, respectively, announce: "If you choose c̄, I will respond with c̄ with probability $1 - p$ [for column]/$1 - q$ [for row]." On the other hand, $1 - s$ is the conditional probability that column will choose c̄ without provocation (that is, after row has chosen c).

This latter probability, I assume, need not be announced. If column says anything, he is likely to say he will never choose c̄ first ("no first use"); this is another way of saying $s = 1$. But the primary basis for choosing c or c̄—whether row or column makes the choice—depends, I assume, on the following comparisons (I consider only those starting on the bottom left-hand side of the game tree since the right-hand side reflects only a possible retaliatory response by column):

---

27. The 2×4 games in figure 1.2 could also be represented in this form, with each of the four (r_i, c_j) payoffs in these games associated with the endpoints of the four bottom branches of the game in figure 1.4.

FIGURE 1.4   Game Tree of Deterrence Game

Row

C   Č

$E_R(C) = r_3s + \{[r_2q + r_1(1 - q)](1 - s)\}$ $E_R(\bar{C}) = r_4p + r_1(1 - p)$

Column   Column

C   Č   C   Č

s $1 - s$ p $1 - p$

$E_C(C) = c_3;$ $E_C(\bar{C}) = c_4q + c_1(1 - q)$ $E_C(C) = c_2;$ $E_C(\bar{C}) = c_1$

Key: E_R = expected payoff to row for choosing C or Č
        E_C = expected payoff to column for choosing C or Č
        p = probability that column chooses C, given row's prior choice of Č
        q = probability that row chooses C, given column's prior choice of Č (and
             row's prior choice of C)
        s = probability that column chooses C, given row's prior choice of C
        C = cooperation; Č = noncooperation

1. The last-moving player (column) will choose C if $E_C(C) >$ $E_C(\bar{C})$, Č if this inequality is reversed.
2. The first-moving player (row) will choose C if $E_R(C) > E_R(\bar{C})$, Č if this inequality is reversed.
3. If these inequalities are equalities, the players will be indifferent between their choices of C and Č.

To illustrate this process of *backward induction*—in which players, working backward from the bottom to the top of the game tree, antici-pate each other's subsequent rational choices—assume row chooses a q such that $E_C(C) > E_C(\bar{C})$ on the bottom left-hand side:

$$c_3 > c_4q + c_1(1 - q). \tag{1.2}$$

This inequality for column is analogous to inequality (1.1) for row (see section 1.3); solving for q yields

$$q < \frac{c_3 - c_1}{c_4 - c_1}. \tag{1.3}$$

Given that (1.3) is satisfied, column's rational choice on the bottom left-hand side of the game tree will be C. Anticipating this choice, row can set $s = 1$, making $E_R(C) = r_3$. Consequently, at the top of the tree, row's choice of C will be rational if column chooses a p such that $r_3 > r_4 p + r_1(1 - p)$. This is inequality (1.1), and solving for p yields

$$p < \frac{r_3 - r_1}{r_4 - r_1}, \qquad (1.4)$$

as shown in section 1.3.

Now the backward-induction process can be reversed, and rational choices, starting at the top of the game tree, can be determined. To wit, if column and row choose p and q such that they satisfy inequalities (1.4) and (1.3), respectively, it is rational for row to choose C initially and for column to respond by choosing c, resulting in the cooperative outcome (r_3, c_3).

Since satisfaction of these inequalities is also sufficient to induce CC if the roles of the players are reversed—column moves first and row responds—*the order of play is immaterial.* Hence, the players in the game shown in figure 1.4 could be interchanged, with the rational choice of CC unaffected as long as both inequalities (1.3) and (1.4) are satisfied.

But what if one or both of these inequalities is not satisfied? Or what if, lacking complete information, one player does not know the payoffs of the other player and, hence, whether his probabilistic threat is sufficient to deter his opponent from choosing c̄? Even given complete information, and probabilistic threats that make the choice of c rational for both players, it is still possible that the choice of c̄—say, an *accidental* nuclear first strike—may occur unprovoked.[28]

1.5. The Preemption Calculation (without Retaliation)

Whatever may induce the first choice of c̄ by a player (say, column on the bottom left-hand side of the game tree in figure 1.4), this possibility must presumably be taken into account by row in his own calculations.

28. The chances of accidental nuclear war, at least between the superpowers, seem extremely unlikely today, but this does not gainsay the need for making "command, control, communications, and intelligence" (C³I) more impregnable and reliable. See Peter Pringle and William Arkin, *SIOP: The Secret U.S. Plan for Nuclear War* (New York: Norton, 1983); Paul Bracken, *The Command and Control of Nuclear Forces* (New Haven: Yale University Press, 1984); and Charles A. Zraket, "Strategic Command, Control, Communications, and Intelligence," *Science* 224 (22 June 1984):1306–11.

If $s \neq 1$, row faces the possibility of being preempted if column chooses $\bar{c}$ first. In light of this possibility, should he preempt column by choosing $\bar{c}$ himself before column does?

This preemption choice would seem a logical response to the immediate incentive each player has to defect from the cooperative (r_3, c_3) outcome, at least in the 2 × 2 version of Chicken in figure 1.3. Yet, in the figure 1.4 version, the player who preempts must consider the consequences of his opponent's retaliating.

Assume, however, for reasons given earlier, that *one* player, if he is preempted, considers it irrational to respond himself and ensure, perhaps, a nuclear holocaust; but the other player indicates a willingness to respond. What should the unwilling player do? (I shall consider the case when both players are willing to retaliate in section 1.6.)

Assume row is the player unwilling to retaliate. If he is preempted, his payoff is r_2. On the other hand, if he preempts column, and column's probability of responding with c is p and with $\bar{c}$ is $1 - p$, then row's expected payoff from preempting column is $r_4 p + r_1(1 - p)$, as shown in figure 1.4.

Clearly, it is rational for row to preempt column if

$$r_4 p + r_1(1 - p) > r_2. \tag{1.5}$$

Note that the left-hand side of this inequality is the same as the right-hand side of inequality (1.1), so these inequalities can be combined:

$$r_2 < r_4 p + r_1(1 - p) < r_3. \tag{1.6}$$

This result may seem curious, for it says that when row's expected payoff from choosing $\bar{c}$ lies between the lower limit of r_2 and the upper limit of r_3, row will be deterred according to inequality (1.1) and will preempt according to inequality (1.5).

The resolution of this apparent contradiction lies in with what row's expected payoff from column's probabilistic threat, $r_4 p + r_1(1 - p)$, is compared: (1) if it is row's payoff from joint cooperation at (r_3, c_3), row will be deterred in the interval given in inequality (1.6); (2) if it is row's payoff from being preempted at (r_2, c_4), he will instead preempt. Perhaps the optimist would say (1) is the proper comparison, whereas the pessimist would say (2) is the proper comparison.

Is there any way of reconciling these different viewpoints? Each seems rooted in a different conception of what the players view as the alternative that the other side is entertaining—for row, either subsequent cooperation by column (and thus r_3 from choosing c first) or preemption by column (and thus r_2 from choosing c first). The problem row faces, if (combined) inequality (1.6) is satisfied, is that his rational course of action depends on which conception is correct: row will choose c if he bases his rational calculation on inequality (1.1), c̄ if he bases it on (1.5).

Of course, if column chooses a p so as to *reverse* inequality (1.5), there will be no problem, because when

$$r_2 > r_4 p + r_1(1 - p), \tag{1.7}$$

a fortiori inequality (1.1) is satisfied, since $r_3 > r_2$. But satisfying inequality (1.7), as opposed to inequality (1.1), requires a higher probability of retaliation, $1 - p$, making column's probabilistic threat less credible (more on this problem later).

So far I have shown that inequality (1.1), which makes it rational for row to be deterred by column's threat, and inequality (1.5), which makes it rational for row to preempt column, yield inconsistent prescriptions in the interval given by inequality (1.6). But when inequality (1.7) is satisfied, there is no inconsistency; then (1.1) and (1.7) prescribe the same strategy for row—namely, choose c—but (1.7) requires that column make the probability of escalation, $1 - p$, higher than does (1.1), should row not cooperate.

Is the price of consistency, and deterrence against the temptation to preempt, a more incredible threat? As I shall shown in section 1.6, even the satisfaction of inequality (1.7), with its more incredible probabilistic threat than that prescribed by the satisfaction of inequality (1.1), may be insufficient to deter one player from trying to preempt the other in Chicken. Even worse, each player's rational attempt may create a situation impossible to realize.

1.6. The Preemption Calculation (with Retaliation): An Impossibility Result

Inequality (1.7), which reverses inequality (1.5), makes it rational for row to be preempted (r_2) rather than preempt and thereby risk his worst possible outcome (r_1). Yet, the game of Chicken is symmetric, and in section 1.5 only the calculation for *one* player's (column's) rational response to preemption was given, under the presumption that the other player (row) would not retaliate if preempted.

The problem with this calculation is that if column thought he could preempt row with impunity, he would do so with great dispatch. And in the race to preempt, he would have an obvious advantage over row, who would have to weigh his expected payoff from preempting against his expected payoff from being preempted to determine whether inequality (1.5) or (1.7) was satisfied. (Even if row had made this calculation in advance, the fact that it may not be rational for him to preempt—and column's knowledge of that—would presumably reinforce column's decision to preempt.) Moreover, if row tried to announce a probabilistic threat that he never intended to carry out, he would confront a number of obstacles in making it credible.

It therefore seems that *both* players would have good reason to threaten each other with retaliation should either preempt. Contrary to the assumption of a one-sided probabilistic threat in section 1.5—in which I assumed column would threaten row but row would not threaten column, or at least would relent on his threat if preempted—it seems logical to suppose that threats in the deterrence game will be two-sided. Indeed, this supposition is reflected in the game tree in figure 1.4, in which, as assumed in section 1.4, row is posited to have a probabilistic threat analogous to column's: if column chooses c̄ first, row will choose c with probability q, c̄ with probability $1 - q$.

Empirically, this assumption seems to describe the mutual threats that enmesh the superpowers today. Unfortunately, as I shall next demonstrate, they lead to a logical impossibility, with potentially grievous consequences, if the superpowers act rationally.

Consider inequality (1.7), whose satisfaction I showed in section 1.5 would be sufficient to deter row from preempting [and simultaneously satisfy the less stringent inequality (1.1)]. My assumption about row's probabilistic threat of choosing c̄ with probability $1 - q$ if preempted entails that the left-hand side of inequality (1.7) not be r_2, which presumes row acquiesces after being preempted, but $r_2q + r_1(1 - q)$, whereby row cooperates if preempted with probability q, escalates the conflict with probability $1 - q$.

Substituting this expected payoff for r_2 in inequality (1.7) yields

$$r_2q + r_1(1 - q) > r_4p + r_1(1 - p). \tag{1.8}$$

Simplifying yields

$$q(r_2 - r_1) > p(r_4 - r_1).$$

Because $r_1 < r_2 < r_4$,

$$p < \left(\frac{r_2 - r_1}{r_4 - r_1}\right)q < q.$$

Therefore, if inequality (1.8) is to be satisfied, $p < q$.

What does this say? Rewrite this inequality as $1 - p > 1 - q$, whose interpretation is that the probability that column will retaliate against preemption ($1 - p$) is greater than row's probability of retaliation ($1 - q$). In other words, column, to deter row, must be *more willing* than row to carry out his threat of retaliation—if row preempts by choosing c̄. But from row's perspective of deterring column, this argument must be reversed: substituting c for r and interchanging p's and q's in inequality (1.8) yields

$$c_2 p + c_1(1 - p) > c_4 q + c_1(1 - q), \tag{1.9}$$

which implies $q < p$.

But now there is a contradiction between the implications of inequalities (1.8) and (1.9): each side must indicate a *greater* probability of retaliation than the other in order to render preemption by his opponent irrational. (I assume such probabilities can be made known and are believed in a game of complete information.) But this is impossible for both sides, simultaneously, to do; hence, there is a contradiction in both sides' making rational probabilistic threats that deter each other.

Although both inequalities (1.8) and (1.9) cannot be satisfied simultaneously, when they are treated as equalities there is a unique solution: $p = q = 0$. This is equivalent to $1 - p = 1 - q = 1$, which says that each player's threat of retaliation is certain, leaving no ambiguity that the threat will be carried out. Indeed, if no possibility of a cooperative response to noncooperative behavior is considered tolerable, a probabilistic threat becomes a deterministic one.

Given that inequalities (1.8) and (1.9) are equalities and retaliation is certain if one's opponent chooses c̄, it may seem paradoxical that row would be indifferent between being preempted and preempting column.

But remember that these choices implacably lead to the same outcome, (r_1, c_1), when retaliation is certain on the part of each player.

The challenge now is to show how the players' rational calculations can lead them away from the grim choice, assumed in this and the previous section, between preempting or being preempted (with or without retaliation by both). To do this, I shall develop a more general model that compares the expected payoff each player suffers from possible retaliation if one chooses $\bar{c}$—the right-hand sides of inequalities (1.8) and (1.9)—with *both* the advantage of cooperation and the possible disadvantages of being preempted. Using this model, I shall demonstrate that the way out of contradiction is a policy that couples probabilistic threats *and* the doctrine of no first use.

1.7. Escape from Impossibility: No First Use

Assume, from row's perspective, that if he chooses c, column will cooperate with probability s, giving him r_3, and not cooperate with probability $1 - s$, giving him $r_2 q + r_1(1 - q)$—because, if preempted, row will choose c with probability q and $\bar{c}$ with probability $1 - q$, as discussed in section 1.4. Row's expected payoff from choosing c, therefore, will be

$$r_3 s + \{[r_2 q + r_1(1 - q)](1 - s)\},$$

which is $E_R(c)$ in figure 1.4.

Now, though, instead of assuming that column will respond to row's choice of c deterministrically—by choosing either c or $\bar{c}$ with certainty, based on a comparison of $E_C(c)$ and $E_C(\bar{c})$ in figure 1.4—I instead assume that column's response will be probabilistic, with s being his probability of choosing c. Moreover, if column chooses $\bar{c}$, row's counterresponse will also be probabilistic, consistent with his probabilistic threat of retaliation, as discussed in section 1.6.

For row to choose c, his expected payoff, as defined in the previous paragraph, must exceed his expected payoff when he preempts by choosing $\bar{c}$ and column responds probabilistically, as defined by the right-hand side of inequality (1.8). In other words, $E_R(c) > E_R(\bar{c})$ in figure 1.4:

$$r_3 s + \{[r_2 q + r_1(1 - q)](1 - s)\} > r_4 p + r_1(1 - p). \quad (1.10)$$

If $k = [r_2 q + r_1(1 - q)]$, then inequality (1.10) becomes

$$r_3 s + k - ks > r_4 p + r_1(1 - p),$$
$$(r_3 - k)s > r_4 p + r_1 - r_1 p - k,$$
$$s > \frac{r_4 p + r_1 - r_1 p - k}{r_3 - k}. \tag{1.11}$$

Now the left-hand side of inequality (1.10) will be maximized when s is as large as possible. But row does not choose s; column does. Neither does row choose the other probability, p, shown in both inequalities (1.10) and (1.11).

Observe, however, that if column chooses p such that the numerator of the right-hand side of inequality (1.11) is equal to the denominator, or

$$(r_4 - r_1)p + r_1 - k = r_3 - k,$$

then

$$p = \frac{r_3 - r_1}{r_4 - r_1}. \tag{1.12}$$

and inequality (1.11) becomes $s > 1$, which is impossible since s is a probability. Accordingly, let $p' = p - \epsilon$, where p is defined by equation (1.12) and ϵ is some arbitrarily small positive number. Then column's choice of a p' slightly less than p will ensure that $s = 1$ satisfies inequality (1.11) and, for all practical purposes, that $s = 1$ is the only probability less than or equal to 1 that does so. Inequality (1.10) can then be rewritten as

$$r_3 > r_4 p' + r_1(1 - p'),$$

which is inequality (1.1) with p' substituted for p.

In other words, the original deterrence condition is justified under the more general model. That is, by assuming that column's response to row's choice of $\bar{c}$ will not necessarily be either c or $\bar{c}$, but some probabilistic mix, I have demonstrated how column can choose his probabilistic threat of retaliation, $1 - p$, to be the lowest value that still induces row to choose c initially. However, this inducement says nothing about what it is in column's interest to do.

Assume column has announced $p = p'$ and made this choice of p credible to row. (I have not included column's announcement in the game tree but assume that his probability of retaliation, $1 - p'$, can somehow be communicated to row and will be believed.) Now row does not know s, but he does know that for him $E_R(c) > E_R(\bar{c})$, given by inequality (1.10), iff (if and only if) $s = 1$, as I just showed, when $p = p'$.

Is it in column's interest to make $s = 1$? If he does, he will realize c_3. But if $s < 1$, column's expected payoff will be

$$c_3 s + \{[c_4 q + c_1(1 - q)](1 - s)\},$$

a probabilistic combination of $E_C(c)$ and $E_C(\bar{c})$, which are shown on the bottom left-hand side of figure 1.4.

But this expected payoff will be less than c_3 if $q = q'$, which is analogous to p' for row. These probabilities are defined by

$$p' = \left(\frac{r_3 - r_1}{r_4 - r_1}\right)^{-} ; q' = \left(\frac{c_3 - c_1}{c_4 - c_1}\right)^{-}, \tag{1.13}$$

where the superscripted minus signs indicate a value slightly less than that given by the parenthetic expressions on the right-hand side of each equation. Since row's choice of q' induces $E_C(c) > E_C(\bar{c})$, it is rational for column always to choose c ($s = 1$).

Hence, given column's credible announcement of p' and row's initial choice of c, it is rational for column to make $s = 1$ and always respond with c himself, leading to (r_3, c_3). The fact that row knows that it is in column's interest always to choose c ($s = 1$)—after row has chosen c—"locks" both players into the rational choice of cc.

This locking in, of course, depends on row's also having a credible threat of retaliation, $1 - q'$, should he be required to respond to column's (irrational) choice of $\bar{c}$ in the figure 1.4 game tree. If the roles of the players are reversed and column should make the initial strategy choice, the previous analysis carries through, with column and row interchanged in the game tree and appropriate changes made in the expected payoffs.

In fact, the order of play is irrelevant to achieving (r_3, c_3), given credible announcements by both players of probabilities of retaliation, $1 - p'$ (for column) and $1 - q'$ (for row). For, in this case, the players will know that there is no penalty in one's going first: it will always be in the other player's interest to respond to his (the first player's) choice of c by choosing c himself. Moreover, as previously shown, these probabilistic threats also ensure that a player's initial choice of $\bar{c}$ is irrational.

To understand, algebraically, how this feat of ensuring CC is rendered rational, consider again inequality (1.10). The right-hand side, reflecting column's probabilistic threat if he is preempted by row, is what column wants to avoid being triggered; he can do this by ensuring that, for himself, $s = 1$ is rational and that row knows this. But to do that, column must manipulate the expected payoff on the right-hand side so that it is not so low that it can be satisfied by $s < 1$ on the left-hand side (because $1 - p$ on the right-hand side is too high) and not so high that it cannot be satisfied by $s = 1$ on the left-hand side (because p on the right-hand side is too high).

In fact, the in-between p that does both of these things is equal to p', slightly less than the p defined by equation (1.12). This, of course, defines column's probabilistic threat, $1 - p'$, which he makes sufficiently high both to deter row and to make it rational for himself always to cooperate (in light of row's threat).

Likewise, row's probabilistic threat, $1 - q'$, is chosen so as to induce column to choose c on the bottom left-hand side of the game tree. Note that these threats, defined by equations (1.13), require information about an opponent's payoffs: column's probabilistic threat depends on row's payoffs, and row's on column's.

In addition, note that both players' threats are perfectly consistent. Unlike the solutions to inequalities (1.8) and (1.9) in section 1.6, which required that each player have a higher threat of retaliation than the other—an impossibility—substitution of p' into inequality (1.10), and of q' into an analogous inequality for column, does not lead to a contradiction.

The reason is that when $p = p'$ on the right-hand side of (1.10), $s = 1$ is effectively the *only* value that satisfies inequality (1.10); since $1 - s = 0$ in this case, the value of the bracketed term on the left-hand side of (1.10)—and, therefore, the value of q—has no bearing on the satisfaction of (1.10). Similarly, satisfying an analogous inequality for column is independent of row's probabilistic threat, so both players' threats can be, without contradiction, solutions in this deterrence game.

Rational play of this game that, for column's choice of $p = p'$ and row's choice of $q = q'$, induces each player always to choose c is equivalent to a *no-first-use policy*—never choose c̄ first.[29] For, starting at the bottom of the game tree in figure 1.4, the fact that column always does better when $s = 1$—and so chooses c—means, at the top of the tree, that row also does better by choosing c, given their probabilistic threats of retaliation, $1 - p'$ and $1 - q'$.

29. See McGeorge S. Bundy, George F. Kennan, Robert S. McNamara, and Gerard Smith, "Nuclear Weapons and the Atlantic Alliance," *Foreign Affairs* 60 (Spring 1982):753–68; John D. Steinbrunner and Leon V. Sigal, eds., *Alliance Security: NATO and the No-First-Use Question* (Washington, DC: Brookings, 1983); and Kurt Gottfried, Henry W. Kendall, and John M. Lee, " 'No First Use' of Nuclear Weapons," *Scientific American* 250, no. 3 (March 1984):33–41. It should be pointed out that "no first use" in the model is applicable only to the superpowers, not to deterring conventional attacks on their allies, for which this policy has most forcefully been advocated. Of course, holding out the possibility of using nuclear weapons first, on a limited basis, as a means to deter conventional war (for example, in Western Europe) is not the same thing as deterring either a limited or full-scale nuclear attack by the Soviet Union against the United States today. (At the dawn of the nuclear age, it is worth noting, there were those who advocated a preemptive attack on Soviet nuclear facilities to prevent their ever developing their own nuclear weapons.) Whether or not a no-first-use pledge buttresses an *overall* policy of nuclear deterrence seems to rest on two contradictory propositions:

1. *Helps:* It reduces the *immediate* risk of nuclear escalation through public commitments of restraint.
2. *Hurts:* It makes conventional war less dangerous and therefore more likely, placing in jeopardy what nuclear deterrence is meant to preserve. In so doing, it increases the *eventual* risk of nuclear war because of the greater probability of escalation in the (more likely) conventional wars that would develop, especially should the position of any country in a conventional war become untenable and it feel it has little to lose by nuclear escalation.

By making conventional war more likely in a region like Western Europe, a no-first-use pledge may also destabilize the Western alliance and undermine extended deterrence (see section 1.1). On this point, see Erich Weede, "Some (Western) Dilemmas in Managing Extended Deterrence" (Forschunginstitut für Soziologie, University of Cologne, 1984, mimeographed), who points out that countries like West Germany, which are at obvious risk should a Soviet invasion occur, have different strategic interests from the United States. In particular, they want the Soviets to know that an attack would trigger nuclear retaliation rather than be met by conventional forces alone, so the Soviets had better reconsider the possible advantages of a conventional attack. This posture, of course, allows for first use of nuclear weapons.

I shall not try to model the possibly opposing effects of a no-first-use pledge but think that this is an important task for future research. At a minimum, these putative effects suggest that there may be a fundamental inconsistency in making deterrence rational *at all levels*.

More specifically, these threats are what ensure that inequality (1.10) and an analogous inequality for column are satisfied. These inequalities reduce to inequalities (1.1) and (1.2), which prescribe the rational choice of CC, when $s = 1$. Thereby defection from the choice of c is rendered unprofitable for both players, so neither will ever choose $\bar{c}$ except, possibly, in response to $\bar{c}$. But this would be retaliation for the other player's prior choice of $\bar{c}$; since $\bar{c}$ is not rational in the first place ($s = 1$), it should never be chosen initially, which is no first use.

1.8. Other Games as Models of Deterrence

Do these solutions make sense in games other than Chicken? In section 1.3 I indicated that only Chicken and Prisoners' Dilemma, among the 78 distinct 2×2 strictly ordinal games, satisfy three criteria; furthermore, I argued that Chicken seemed better to capture the threats implicit in deterrence. In light of the development of the deterrence model so far, is that judgment still sensible?

I believe it is. Recall that Prisoners' Dilemma involves interchanging the two worst payoffs, r_1 and r_2, in Chicken. Now if r_2 is substituted for r_1 in (1.10) and vice versa, the left-hand side of (1.10) will be maximized, as before, when $s = 1$; and probabilistic threats, analogous to those given by (1.13) with this substitution of r_1 and r_2 made, would appear to be optimal for column and row, respectively.

But recall that if row preempts in Prisoners' Dilemma, forcing upon column his worst outcome, it is rational for column *always* to respond with $\bar{c}$, making the right-hand side of (1.10), with r_2 in place of r_1, r_2. Similarly, if, after row chooses c, column responds with $\bar{c}$, it is rational for row always to counterrespond with $\bar{c}$, making the bracketed term on the left-hand side of equation (1.10) simply r_2. These two emendations in (1.10) for Prisoners' Dilemma give

$$r_3 s + r_2(1 - s) > r_2, \tag{1.14}$$

which is always satisfied, except when $s = 0$ [when (1.14) is an equality].

In other words, there is no "need" for probabilistic threats in Prisoners' Dilemma, because the players, acting rationally, will "automatically" ensure that inequality (1.14) is satisfied. To be sure, to the extent that column always cooperates when row does ($s = 1$), or says he will, row can rest better assured that (1.14) will be satisfied and he should cooperate, too. But a threat, probabilistic or deterministic, seems quite unnecessary in the case of Prisoners' Dilemma, because it is rational for each player always to respond to his opponent's choice of $\bar{c}$ with the choice of $\bar{c}$ himself, and both players know this.

Indeed, because $\bar{c}$ is each player's dominant strategy in Prisoners' Dilemma, the choice of $\bar{c}$ by both, leading to the Pareto-inferior outcome (r_2, c_2), would appear hard to avoid. Yet, insofar as each player anticipates that the other will respond cooperatively to his choice of c (with probability $s > 0$), inequality (1.14) is satisfied. This renders row's initial choice of c rational, for his choice of $\bar{c}$, by assumption, would inevitably lead to r_2; so would column's response of $\bar{c}$ (with probability $1 - s$) to row's initial choice of C, thereby making $s = 1$ rational for both column and row.

I do not mean to imply, however, that Prisoner's Dilemma does not pose a true dilemma for the players. Rather, what I have tried to show is that the notion of a probabilistic threat, and expected-payoff calculations based on such a threat, seem largely irrelevant in this game.

To be sure, the left-hand side of inequality (1.10) is an expected payoff, so such calculations certainly can be made for Prisoners' Dilemma with threats. But the bracketed expected payoff reflecting row's probabilistic threat in inequality (1.10), which is reduced to r_2 in (1.14), renders the deterrence model—as so far developed—vacuous in the case of Prisoners' Dilemma: once one player chooses $\bar{c}$, the other player need not equivocate about his rational choice in this game—to respond with $\bar{c}$ himself. On the other hand, I shall argue in chapter 3 that Prisoners' Dilemma serves well as a model of the superpower arms race, in which each side can detect, with a specified probability, the strategy choice of the other side.

1.9. MAD and the Problem of Credibility

A policy of MAD, whereby $p = 0$ and $q = 0$ (threats of retaliation are a certainty), also satisfies inequality (1.10) if $s > 0$:

$$r_3 s + r_1(1 - s) > r_1.$$

That is, as long as there is some nonzero probability s, however small, that a player's choice of c will not always be exploited by the other's choice of $\bar{c}$, it pays to choose c initially.

But will column, given his choice on the left-hand side of the figure

1.4 game tree, choose c̄? In fact, he will choose c if $E_C(c) > E_C(c̄)$, which is inequality (1.2) and whose solution is any q satisfying inequality (1.3).

In other words, $p = q = 0$, or a policy of MAD, is certainly *not* required to induce the choice of c by the players in the figure 1.4 deterrence game. Row will choose c because it *is* rational for column to respond with c as long as $q \leq q'$, given by equation (1.13), and always so $(s = 1)$ if $q = q'$. Likewise, if row chooses a $p \leq p'$, it is rational for column to choose c, too.

Thus, while p' and q' are sufficient to induce the cooperative outcome CC, as I showed earlier, they are not the only values that "work." In effect, they provide a threshold above which deterrence fails and below which it succeeds (because the probabilities of retaliation, $1 - p'$ and $1 - q'$ for column and row, respectively, are sufficiently high). Put another way, one can afford to choose c, even initially, as long as one holds out a rational threat of responding with c̄ if one's opponent does not choose c also.

The innovation in this analysis, I believe, is to show that these threats need not be deterministic, and hence quite incredible. Instead, they can be probabilistic—making one's response uncertain—as long as the probabilities of retaliation are sufficiently high.

Of course, it may be neither feasible nor advisable to try to tailor probabilistic threats so that they *just* deter an adversary. For one thing, since the threshold probabilities depend on the payoffs of one's opponent, about which one may possess only limited information, such "fine-tuning" may not even be possible. This difficulty may well attenuate the advantage of choosing a level (for column, choosing a p') that induces him always to choose c $(s = 1)$ so that row, in turn, knows that he should also choose c because $E_R(c) > E_R(c̄)$.

Recall from inequality (1.10) that an infinite number of $p < p'$ (including $p = 0$) satisfy this inequality and thereby induce row to cooperate. But only $p = p'$ forces $s = 1$ in order that (1.10) be satisfied, which ensures that column, too, will always cooperate.

When this is not the case because, say, row follows a policy of MAD $(p = 0)$, column can satisfy (1.10) with any $s > 0$, which may well induce him not to assure row he will always cooperate.[30] Row, in turn,

---

30. But if uncertainty is rife, perhaps in part because of the possibility of accidental nuclear war, column probably should offer this assurance by announcing $s = 1$ to drama-

if he thinks column might preempt, has less of an incentive to cooperate in the first place, leading, possibly, to escalating threats that narrow the options to the two of preempting or being preempted. Then, as I showed in section 1.6, no level of threats can succeed in preventing the choice of c̄c̄.

The choice of an appropriate probabilistic threat may run amok of other problems. Recall that the threshold probabilities of retaliation, $1 - p'$ and $1 - q'$, are a function only of the payoffs of one's opponent, whereas credibility is a function of the damage to oneself in carrying out a threat. Because a policy of MAD, subscribed to by both players ($p = q = 0$), may result in "unnecessary" damage to oneself—as well as one's opponent—if deterrence fails, one presumably wants to choose the least damaging probabilistic threat that does not jeopardize deterrence.

In the intervals $0 \leq p \leq p'$ and $0 \leq q \leq q'$, the effectiveness of one's threat increases at the same time that one's credibility declines as the players move toward $p = q = 0$. In theory, of course, p' and q' are sufficient to deter one's opponent; call this threat a *credible threat,* whose effectiveness is minimal. By contrast, an *effective threat* is one whose credibility is minimal—that is, $p = q = 0$, consistent with a policy of MAD.

Whether a threat is credible, effective, or somewhere in between, it would appear to pose a problem for the threatener in carrying it out. After all, once one player has chosen c̄, the other player *always* does worse in responding with c̄, either on a probabilistic basis (in terms of his expected payoff) or a deterministic basis (in terms of a certain payoff). Hence, such a threat cannot lead to what is called a "perfect equilibrium," because it would be irrational to implement it.[31]

There is an element of irrationality in such a threat, however, only if a player can make a completely free choice after his opponent chooses c̄. But, as I shall argue in section 1.11, operational procedures that are

---

tize the difference between $E_R(c)$ and $E_R(\bar{c})$. For an extension of this model, see Steven J. Brams and D. Marc Kilgour, "Optimal Deterrence" (Department of Politics, New York University, 1984, mimeographed).

31. A *perfect equilibrium* is an outcome that is in equilibrium in every subgame of an extensive-form game. For a formal development of this concept with examples, and a discussion of extensions that have been made in it, see Martin Shubik, *Game Theory in the Social Sciences: Concepts and Solutions* (Cambridge, MA: MIT Press, 1982), pp. 265–70.

set in motion if one superpower attacks another not only constrain choices; they also render a deterministic threat by the superpower attacked a probabilistic one and thereby make it more credible.

Nevertheless, it would still seem irrational to carry out even a probabilistic threat in the deterrence game in figure 1.4. Yet, if the attacker knows that the attacked cannot countermand procedures for (possibly) carrying out this threat—because it is controlled by a (probabilistic) "doomsday machine," whose response is automatic—the attacker cannot bank on the imperfectness of the resulting equilibrium.

There may, therefore, be a logic to building an irreversibility into the implementation of an imperfect equilibrium. For if mandating an "irrational" response of $\bar{c}$ is a necessary (but not sufficient) condition to deter an opponent from initially choosing $\bar{c}$, then it may be rational, even should deterrence sometimes fail and the doomsday machine be set in motion.

Put another way, one threatens a nonmaximizing choice that flouts one's preferences as part of a deterrence policy that one thinks will (ultimately) maximize one's (expected) payoff. If adoption of the deterrence policy influences an opponent's rational strategy in a way favorable to oneself, there may be a good reason for risking a costly reprisal. The alternative to eschewing all threat behavior, in bluntest terms, "can only be the willingness to accept victimization, to suffer passively a nuclear strike, or to acquiesce in whatever the potential striker demands as the price of its avoidance."[32]

1.10. Robust Threats

Probabilistic threats p' and q' given by equations (1.13), which "just" satisfy inequalities (1.3) and (1.4), have a serious shortcoming: they possess a dangerous knife-edge quality, making a slight underestimation of the probabilities of retaliation, $1 - p'$ and $1 - q'$, possibly fatal in the deterrence game. This may occur because small misperceptions may lead one or both players to believe that inequalities (1.3) or (1.4)

---

32. Gauthier, "Deterrence, Maximization, and Rationality," p. 494; for other examples of the strange twists that rationality may produce, see Jon Elster, *Ulysses and the Sirens: Studies in Rationality and Irrationality* (Cambridge: Cambridge University Press, 1979).

FIGURE 1.5   2 × 2 Deterrence Game

Column

	c	c̄

		c	c̄
Row	c	(r_3, c_3)	$(r_2 q + r_1[1 - q],$ $c_4 q + c_1[1 - q])$
	c̄	$(r_4 p + r_1[1 - p],$ $c_2 p + c_1[1 - p]),$	(r_1, c_1)

Key: (r_i, c_j) = (payoff to row, payoff to column)
  r_4, c_4 = best payoffs; r_3, c_3 = next-best payoffs; r_2, c_2 = next-worst payoffs; r_1, c_1 = worst payoffs
  p = probability that column stays at c, given that row chose c̄ and that column chose c initially
  q = probability that row stays at c, given that column chose c̄ and that row chose c initially
  c = cooperation; c̄ = noncooperation

are reversed and the choice of c̄, therefore, is rational. MAD, if incredible, may be safer.

Are there rational probabilistic threats not on the knife edge that, at the same time, do not push one in the opposite direction toward incredible pronouncements? Consider the 2 × 2 game shown in figure 1.5, which is equivalent to the figure 1.4 game tree if one presumes that row does *not* choose first—or that column chooses in ignorance of row's choice—and vice versa. Then each player may escalate (choose c̄) if the other chose c̄.[33]

Recall that I showed in section 1.4 that if inequalities (1.3) and (1.4) are satisfied, the choice of c by both players is rational, leading to (r_3, c_3), whichever player is assumed to choose first in the figure 1.4 game tree. As long as these inequalities are satisfied in figure 1.5, in which the players are assumed to make simultaneous strategy choices

33. In fact, row is depicted as making the first choice in figure 1.4, and column, knowing row's choice, as then responding to it. However, if column were assumed not to know column's initial choice, this would be indicated in figure 1.4 by enclosing his two choices, at the endpoints of each of row's branches, in the same "information set." For a description and analysis of such sets, see Steven J. Brams, *Game Theory and Politics* (New York: Free Press, 1975), pp. 8–11.

initially but then (possibly) escalate according to p or q if the other player chose $\bar{c}$, the choice of c is also rational because it is a dominant strategy for each player. In row's case, for example, inequality (1.4) ensures that he prefers the outcome associated with c to $\bar{c}$ if column chooses c; if column chooses $\bar{c}$, c still leads to an outcome at least as good (if $q = 0$) and in general better (if $q > 0$).

The dominance of c for each player not only guarantees that c is in general better for each—whether his opponent chooses c or $\bar{c}$—but also that (r_3, c_3) is a mutually best outcome. This means that probabilistic threats can transform Chicken as shown in figure 1.3, in which neither player has a dominant strategy and (r_3, c_3) is only a next-best outcome for both, into a new game that makes the choice of c by both players far more attractive.

It is important to note that the valuation of (r_3, c_3) has not changed in the new game. Instead, probabilistic threats have downgraded valuations of the two off-diagonal outcomes in this game. As a result, (r_3, c_3) emerges, in relative terms, as the best outcome when inequalities (1.3) and (1.4) are satisfied.

The satisfaction of these inequalities that makes c a dominant strategy for both players also occurs under MAD, but with one significant difference: when retaliation is certain ($p = q = 0$), all outcomes in the figure 1.5 payoff matrix except (r_3, c_3) become transformed into (r_1, c_1).

When the two off-diagonal outcomes assume these values, *either* player's choice of $\bar{c}$ ensures (r_1, c_1). If one player makes this choice, therefore, it makes no difference to the other player whether his adversary chooses c or $\bar{c}$. This means that, under MAD, c is not unequivocally better than $\bar{c}$. Because cooperation is definitely better only if the other player also cooperates, c is said to dominate $\bar{c}$, but not "strictly."

A *strictly dominant* strategy is *always* better, whatever the other player's choice. On the other hand, a policy of what might be called *minimal deterrence*, given by credible threats p' and q' of equations (1.13), gives strict dominance, but it has the undesirable knife-edge quality alluded to earlier.

Define *robust strategies* to be strategies that

1. are strictly dominant (unlike MAD); and
2. do not have a knife-edge quality (unlike minimal deterrence).

Clearly, there are an infinite number of values of p and q that are neither "minimal" nor "maximal" (à la MAD). Although there is nothing unreasonable in recommending a range of choices, a third condition narrows down this range in a manner, I think, that has striking appeal. More specifically, define *robust deterrence strategies* to be strategies that satisfy both conditions for a robust strategy and a third condition for both players in the figure 1.5 deterrence game:

3. they *equalize* the difference in value of C over C̄ for one's opponent, whatever strategy one chooses (or he thinks one will choose).

In other words, robust deterrence strategies ensure that each player will suffer the same loss in switching from (dominant strategy) C to (dominated strategy) C̄, whatever strategy his opponent chooses. This is not true of MAD: row's loss is $r_3 - r_1 > 0$ if his opponent chooses C, $r_1 - r_1 = 0$ if his opponent chooses C̄. Neither is it true of minimal deterrence: row's loss is $r_3 - [r_4 p' + r_1(1 - p')]$ if his opponent chooses C, $[r_2 q' - r_1(1 - q')] - r_1$ if his opponent chooses C̄; in general, the first loss will be minuscule but the second will not.

To equalize these losses, it is necessary for column to choose a p and for row to choose a q that equalize the differences given in the previous sentence [instead of choosing values p' and q' given by equations (1.13)]:

$$r_3 - [r_4 p + r_1(1 - p)] = [r_2 q - r_1(1 - q)] - r_1.$$

Normalizing, as before, the payoffs by letting $r_1 = 0$ and $r_4 = 1$ for row, and $c_1 = 0$ and $c_4 = 1$ for column, the equalization conditions for the two players are:

$$r_3 - p = r_2 q; \tag{1.16}$$

$$c_3 - q = c_2 p; \tag{1.17}$$

Note that the condition for the deterrence of row (and a similar one for column), inequality (1.4), or $p < r_3$, is satisfied by any p satisfying (1.16), or

$$p = r_3 - r_2 q, \tag{1.18}$$

if $q \neq 0$, which (1.17) requires (as I shall show in the next paragraph).

Substituting the value of p given by equation (1.18) into equation (1.17), it is easy to show that q can be expressed in terms of the intermediate payoffs (r_2 and r_3, c_2 and c_3) of both players:

$$q = \frac{c_3 - c_2 r_3}{1 - c_2 r_2}. \tag{1.19}$$

Clearly, since the denominator of equation (1.19) is always greater than the numerator, $0 < q < 1$. Analogously for column,

$$p = \frac{r_3 - r_2 c_3}{1 - r_2 c_2}. \tag{1.20}$$

Given that column chooses a p and row a q that satisfy equations (1.19) and (1.20), the common loss (L) row faces in switching from c to c̄ is given by substituting equation (1.20) into the right-hand side of equation (1.17):

$$L_R = \frac{c_2(r_3 - r_2 c_3)}{1 - r_2 c_2}. \tag{1.21}$$

If the players value the outcomes in the same manner, so $c_2 = r_2$ and $c_3 = r_3$, then

$$L_R = L_C = \frac{r_2 r_3 (1 - r_2)}{(1 - r_2)(1 + r_2)} = \frac{r_2 r_3}{1 + r_2}, \tag{1.22}$$

which is necessarily less than $\frac{1}{2}$.

Equalizing the losses for both players in switching from c to c̄, whether they value the outcomes in the same manner or not, depends on solving equations (1.16) and (1.17) *simultaneously* for p and q, as given by equations (1.19) and (1.20). If only, say, column chooses his probabilistic threat according to (1.16), but row does not choose his according to (1.17), then column's p will depend on row's q, as given by equation (1.18).

If row adheres to MAD, for example, and therefore sets $q = 0$, then $p = r_3$ according to equation (1.18), which is not even sufficient for minimal deterrence. The fact that this choice of p by column equalizes row's losses (exactly 0!) in switching from c to c̄, whatever strategy column chooses, is small comfort if it only succeeds in robbing row's c strategy of its dominant status [because $p = r_3$, not less than r_3, as required by equation (1.4) with normalization].

The two players can pursue robust deterrence strategies *independently* by not making their strategies dependent on the other player's probabilistic threat but instead on the payoffs, as given by equations

(1.19) and (1.20). To demonstrate this, consider again the simultaneous solutions to equations (1.16) and (1.17) given by equations (1.19) and (1.20). If column chooses p according to equation (1.20), the following calculation about the consequences of column's switching from c to c̄ is pertinent for row:

1. Row chooses c: loss for column of $c_3 - q$;
2. Row chooses c̄: loss for column of $c_2 p = c_2 \left(\dfrac{r_3 - r_2 c_3}{1 - r_2 c_2} \right)$.

To equalize these two losses for column, it is easy to show that row should choose precisely the q given by equation (1.19).

In other words, if only one player chooses a robust strategy according to equation (1.19) or (1.20), the other player can do no better, in constructing a response that equalizes the *other* player's losses in switching from c to c̄, than choose his own robust strategy according to the *other* equation [(1.19) or (1.20)] in the pair. Thus, neither player has anything to fear from choosing his robust strategy at the outset: the other player cannot exploit this information and do still better—in the sense of widening the (equal) gap between payoffs associated with c and c̄ for his opponent—knowing his opponent's (robust) strategy choice. Hence, each's robust strategy is best against the other's in equalizing the loss in switching from c to c̄ for the other player.

I have shown that the simultaneous solution of equations (1.16) and (1.17) that leads to equations (1.19) and (1.20) can be pursued independently by each player, using *only* information about the original payoffs of Chicken and not about the other player's probabilistic threat. If each, by contrast, responds to the other player's threat according to equations (1.16) and (1.17), this leads to a (nonsimultaneous) solution in which robustness may vanish, or deterrence may fail, as I showed in the case of MAD.

So far I have assumed that column will be motivated to choose a p to equalize row's losses, and row a q to equalize column's losses, when each's opponent switches from c to c̄. Recall from section 1.3 that the effectiveness of column's threat to row, *Eff*(c), is the loss that row incurs when column chooses c and he switches from c to c̄. If deterrent strategies are robust, the loss to row will be the same, *whichever* strategy column chooses. Similarly, row's threat to column will be equally damaging to column whichever strategy row chooses.

The (equal) effectiveness of the players' robust strategies, however, is only one side of the coin. Their incredibility, which for row is $Inc(c)$ $= c_3 - c_2 p$ when column chooses C, needs also to be considered.

If column chooses $\bar{c}$, the difference in payoffs for column, should row switch to $\bar{c}$, is q. Equating these differences, $c_3 - c_2 p$ and q, gives, after rearrangement of terms, exactly equation (1.17). Similarly, equation (1.16) is obtained when the "incredibility" differences are set equal for row. As before, the simultaneous solution of these equations is given by equations (1.19) and (1.20).

Remarkably, then, if the players set out to equalize the incredibility differences in the figure 1.5 deterrence game, which are the costs *they themselves* incur when the other player switches from C to $\bar{c}$, each would choose the same p or q that equalizes the effectiveness differences, which are the costs *each inflicts on the other player* when he switches. Thus, at the same time that the player's robust deterrent strategies equalize the damage to the other player from switching, they equalize the damage they themselves incur from the same switch.

A probabilistic threat of some kind of dire reprisal, such as nuclear retaliation, may be considered equivalent to a *certain* threat with less catastrophic consequences, or other threats with different odds. Although some kinds of retaliation may be all-or-nothing, and possibly can only be threatened in terms of the likelihood that they will be used in response to different forms of aggression, other kinds may be capable of being tailored to the nature of the aggression.

What has been called by Kahn an "escalation ladder" indicates what, in his opinion, are gradable levels of hostile behavior.[34] Even in superpower crises as severe as the 1962 Cuban missile crisis (see chapter 2), the United States never considered escalation to nuclear weapons as inevitable, though it has always been considered a grave danger.

Grave as this danger is, in conflicts with each other the superpowers have so far resorted to means short of nuclear war to settle their differences at lower rungs of the escalation ladder. These means have often included what may be considered probabilistic threats. But physical moves, such as those precipitated by the Cuban missile crisis and the 1973 crisis alert (the latter is also described in chapter 2), may in fact

---

34. Herman Kahn, *On Escalation: Metaphors and Scenarios* (New York: Praeger, 1965). These levels of hostile behavior are modeled in Brams and Kilgour, "Optimal Deterrence."

be interpreted as probabilistic threats. In terms of expected value, they are the certain equivalent of a probabilistic threat, lying between, for row, r_4 and r_1 (threat by column to deter row from preempting), or r_2 and r_1 (threat by row, should column preempt him).

These are retaliatory actions that move one up the escalation ladder, but the damage they cause falls short of the disastrous $(1,1)$ outcome in Chicken. As harbingers of onerous events that may unfold, they are intended to evoke fear that will, in the end, halt the most fearsome event—unleashing nuclear war—from occurring. Based on the foregoing analysis, I think there are better and worse ways of doing this, which I shall review in the final section. Given Draper's contention that "short of abolishing nuclear weapons forever and everywhere, deterrence is all we have,"[35] we must, I believe, try to make the best of an unenviable situation to stave off nuclear war.

1.11. Conclusions

The crisis of rationality underlying deterrence is having to carry out a threat that may cause great damage to oneself. I suggested one way around this crisis was to define an ongoing series of games. In such games, a short-term loss might be more than counterbalanced by the enhanced credibility one would enjoy in future games from having demonstrated one's willingness, by carrying out a threat, to incur such a loss in the face of aggrandizement.

This is not a completely satisfactory resolution if carrying out a threat leads to something as unthinkable and irredeemable as nuclear war between the superpowers, which probably would occur only once. Unlike deterrence in a conventional conflict—between, say, a superpower and a smaller country without nuclear weapons, in which one's willingness to carry out a threat will affect one's reputation in future conflicts—credibility in a game without a sequel is purely academic.

The resolution proposed by Zagare seems no less satisfactory: defining deterrence to be a game in which escalation, for the player preempted, is always rational.[36] Escalation is always rational in Prisoners' Dilemma, which, along with Chicken, is the only game that

35. Theodore Draper, *Present History* (New York: Random House, 1983), p. 28.

36. Zagare, "Toward a Reconciliation of Game Theory and the Theory of Mutual Deterrence."

meets criteria that seem to characterize the conflict of interests inherent in deterrence.

Although Chicken better models the rationality crisis implicit in deterrence, it also seems inadequate unless threats can be explicitly modeled in a more realistic representation of this game. To accomplish this, an extensive-form, or game-tree, representation of Chicken was defined that allows the players to make probabilistic threats. Given that the two player's know each other's payoffs, these threats enable each to choose threshold probabilities just sufficient to deter the other player, which I argued are more credible because they do not indicate with certainty that a player will make an apparently irrational choice.

From this game-theoretic model of threats, and a related model embedded in a 2 × 2 deterrence game, a number of conclusions were derived:

1. If a player is in fact unwilling to retaliate but is willing to preempt, his opponent, to try to deter preemption, must indicate his intention to retaliate to be more likely than his threshold probability. At the new retaliatory threshold, the potential preemptor is rendered indifferent between being defeated by attack and preempting himself (instead of being indifferent between mutual cooperation and preemption).
2. If both players view their options as either preempt or be preempted, each must make his threat of retaliation more likely than his opponent's, which is an impossibility.
3. If both players view cooperation as one alternative, then the threshold probabilities that make it rational for neither to attack are equivalent to a policy of no first use (that is, of not attacking first).
4. A policy of MAD, in which retaliation is certain, also is sufficient to deter but it strains credibility; moreover, certain retaliation does not make C strictly dominant in the deterrence game. On the other hand, when information about one's opponent's payoffs is incomplete, MAD provides additional insurance that makes it rational for the players to cooperate.
5. Insofar as MAD appears to be an incredible threat, and is therefore viewed as unlikely to be carried out—even though, if carried out, it will cause great damage and therefore be effective—

there is a trade-off between effectiveness and credibility: the more of one, the less of the other.

6. Robust deterrent threats, which equalize the damage to the threatenee when he switches to $\bar{c}$—whatever strategy the threatener chooses—also equalize the costs to the threatener from such a switch. Being insensitive to the choice of the threatener in terms of both effectiveness and incredibility, they would seem to have advantages over MAD. Although robustness requires that both players make interdependent probabilistic threats, a player cannot be hurt by his opponent's knowledge of this choice.

Although probabilistic threats, whether they are robust or something else, may be more credible than MAD—and still be effective—how can one make them *real*? Obviously, the United States is not about to tell the Soviet Union that it will respond to a major provocation by flipping a coin, whether fair or biased. Not only would such a statement smack of utter foolishness, but it might well erode—rather than strengthen—the credibility of one's threat: would a suicidal course of action *really* be taken if the coin said it should be?

In fact, I believe, significant uncertainty is already built into both the United States' and the Soviet Union's likely response to such a provocation because of a number of operational factors, including problems related to identifying the attacker, identifying the magnitude of the attack, failures of weapons being used for the first time on a massive scale, problems of communication and control, lack of resolve, and the like.[37] In light of these difficulties, both sides have, not surprisingly, resorted less to making probabilistic threats and more to employing

---

37. Such factors are modeled in Claudio Cioffi-Revilla, "A Probability Model of Credibility," *Journal of Conflict Resolution* 27, no. 1 (March 1983):73–108; and Zeev Maoz, "Resolve, Capabilities, and the Outcomes of Interstate Disputes, 1816–1976," *Journal of Conflict Resolution* 27, no. 2 (June 1983):195–229. A description of factors that contribute to the unreliability of a first strike is given in Matthew Bunn and Kosta Tsipis, "The Uncertainties of a Preemptive Nuclear Attack," *Scientific American* 249, no. 5 (November 1983):38–47. Uncertainty, it is important to note, may strengthen, not undermine, nuclear deterrence: "The ambiguity over command of nuclear weapons may actually contribute to the credibility of the NATO deterrent, since it makes it all but impossible to predict the outcome of a crisis that involves the alerting of military forces." Bracken, *Command and Control of Nuclear Forces*, p. 172.

their certain equivalents—usually, controlled steps up the escalation ladder.

These, as I argued earlier, may be thought of as probabilistic threats insofar as they give an opponent a better idea of how close each side is moving toward full-scale retaliation—that is, they indicate more palpably the probability that the opponent will indeed carry out a threat and what its expected damage will be. So far, fortunately, these probabilistic threats have been sufficient to persuade the two sides to back off, beyond a certain point, from continued escalation.

As I shall show in the case studies in chapter 2, this point has created much fear and anxiety when the two sides have approached the precipice. Yet, that is exactly what deterrence is intended to do to forestall catastrophe.

The great danager, of course, is that when threats escalate the two sides will see their options narrowed to preempt or be preempted—leading to the impossible situation described under conclusion 2 above. An intellectual understanding that robust threats may well do the job—and also be more credible—I hope might enable both sides to abandon thoughts of preemption and realize that there are better alternatives that are supported by hard-headed, yet reasonable, calculations devoid of bombast and jingoism.

In fact, as I have argued, MAD—in operational terms—is almost certainly a probabilistic threat. What seems less appreciated is that such threats, especially those that are robust, seem well designed to combine effectiveness and credibility.

2 Deterrence in Two Crises

2.1. Introduction

I turn in this chapter from the realm of theory to that of applications, though I shall also introduce new theory to try to illuminate the applications. The two cases studied are the well-known Cuban missile crisis of 1962 and the less well known crisis between the superpowers that erupted in 1973. The latter crisis was precipitated by President Richard Nixon's decision to put United States military forces on worldwide alert in an attempt to forestall Soviet intervention on the side of Egypt, and bring about a cease-fire, in the so-called Yom Kippur War.

Both crises were resolved peacefully, but they generated much tension between the superpowers, especially the 1962 crisis How the superpowers—or, more accurately, their leaders—managed these crises has been described in great detail, but this scrutiny has involved little in the way of formal and systematic strategic analysis.

I hope not only to shed light on these crises, using game theory, but also to explore how classical game theory can be revised so as to capture the flow of moves by players over time. The founders of game theory recognized that their theory was a static one.[1] By reformulating assumptions of this theory, I shall show how the sequential calculations of

1. John von Neumann and Oskar Morgenstern, *Theory of Games and Economic Behavior*, 3d ed. (Princeton, NJ: Princeton University Press, 1953), pp. 44–45.

players, as they look ahead and try to anticipate consequences of their actions, can be modeled.

Much of this chapter, therefore, will be theoretical, though I hope not so large a portion that the modeling of the two crises, and how deterrent strategies worked in each, will be lost to the reader. An important lesson of such empirical analysis, I believe, is that there is generally no single "correct" view of a situation. In fact, alternative perspectives will be presented on each crisis to illuminate different interpretations to which each is open.

The theory developed in this chapter differs in fundamental ways from the mostly probabilistic theory of the previous chapter. Although it enables one to analyze more completely the dynamics of strictly ordinal games, at the same time it glosses over expected-payoff calculations players might make in real-life games. In later chapters, I shall return to these probabilistic and quantitative considerations in the game-theoretic analysis.

2.2. The Cuban Missile Crisis as a Game of Chicken

Probably the most dangerous confrontation between major powers ever to occur was that between the United States and the Soviet Union in October 1962. This confrontation, in what has come to be known as the Cuban missile crisis, was precipitated by a Soviet attempt to install in Cuba medium-range and intermediate-range nuclear-armed ballistic missiles capable of hitting a large portion of the United States.[2]

After the presence of such missiles was confirmed on October 14, the Central Intelligence Agency estimated that they would be operational in about ten days. A so-called Executive Committee of high-level officials was convened to decide on a course of action for the United States, and the Committee met in secret for six days. Several alternative were considered, which were eventually narrowed to the two that I shall discuss.

The most common conception of this crisis is that the two super-powers were on a collision course. Chicken (section 2.2), which derives its name from a "sport" in which two drivers race toward each

---

2. This section and the next are drawn from Steven J. Brams, "Deception in 2 × 2 Games," *Journal of Peace Science* 2 (Spring 1977):171–203.

FIGURE 2.1   Cuban Missile Crisis as a Game of Chicken

| | | Soviet Union | |
		Withdrawal (w)	Maintenance (m)
United States	Blockade (b)	(3,3) Compromise	(2,4) Soviet victory, U.S. defeat
	Air strike (a)	(4,2) U.S. victory, Soviet defeat	(1,1) Nuclear war

Key: (x,y) = (rank of United States, rank of Soviet Union)
4 = best; 3 = next best; 2 = next worst; 1 = worst

other on a narrow road, would at first blush seem an appropriate model of this conflict.

Under this interpretation, each player has the choice between swerving, and avoiding a head-on collision, or continuing on the collision course. As applied to the Cuban missile crisis, with the United States and the Soviet Union the two players, the alternative courses of action, and a ranking of the players' outcomes in terms of the game of Chicken, are shown in figure 2.1.[3]

The goal of the United States was immediate removal of the Soviet missiles, and United States policymakers seriously considered two alternative courses of action to achieve this end:

1. A naval blockade (b), or "quarantine" as it was euphemistically called, to prevent shipment of further missiles, possibly followed by stronger action to induce the Soviet Union to withdraw those missiles already installed.
2. A "surgical" air strike (a) to wipe out the missiles already installed, insofar as possible, perhaps followed by an invasion of the island.

3. Henceforth I shall assume in this crisis, as in the 1973 alert decision, that the superpowers can be considered unitary actors, though this is an obvious simplification. It is rectified in part by constructing other models that emphasize different features, as Allison has done. Graham T. Allison, *Essence of Decision: Explaining the Cuban Missile Crisis* (Boston: Little, Brown, 1971).

The alternatives open to Soviet policymakers were:

1. Withdrawal (w) of their missiles.
2. Maintenance (m) of their missiles.

Needless to say, the strategy choices and probable outcomes as presented in figure 2.1 provide only a skeletal picture of the crisis as it developed over a period of thirteen days. Both sides considered more than the two alternatives I have listed, as well as several variations on each. The Soviets, for example, demanded withdrawal of American missiles from Turkey as a quid pro quo for withdrawal of their missiles from Cuba, a demand publicly ignored by the United States. Furthermore, there is no way to verify that the outcomes given in figure 2.1 were "probable," or valued in a manner consistent with the game of Chicken. For example, if the Soviet Union had viewed an air strike on their missiles as jeopardizing their vital national interests, the AW outcome may very well have ended in nuclear war between the two sides, giving it the same value as AM. Still another simplification relates to the assumption that the players choose their actions simultaneously, when in fact a continuous exchange in both words and deeds occurred over those fateful days in October.

Nevertheless, most observers of this crisis believe the two superpowers were on a collision course, which is actually the title of one book recounting this nuclear confrontation.[4] Most observers also agree that neither side was eager to take any irreversible step, such as the driver in a game of Chicken might do by defiantly ripping off his steering wheel in full view of his adversary, thereby foreclosing his alternative of swerving.

Although in one sense the United States "won" by getting the Soviets to withdraw their missiles, Premier Khrushchev at the same time extracted from President Kennedy a promise not to invade Cuba,

---

4. Henry M. Pachter, *Collision Course: The Cuban Missile Crisis and Coexistence* (New York: Praeger, 1963). Other books on this crisis include Elie Abel, *The Missile Crisis* (Philadelphia: Lippincott, 1966); Allison, *Essence of Decision;* Robert F. Kennedy, *Thirteen Days: A Memoir of the Cuban Missile Crisis* (New York: Norton, 1969); Robert A. Divine, ed., *The Cuban Missile Crisis* (Chicago: Quadrangle, 1971); Abram Chayes, *The Cuban Missile Crisis: International Crises and the Role of Law* (New York: Oxford University Press, 1974); Herbert Dinerstein, *The Making of the Cuban Missile Crisis, October 1962* (Baltimore: Johns Hopkins University Press, 1976); and David Detzer, *The Brink: Story of the Cuban Missile Crisis* (New York: Crowell, 1979).

which seems to indicate that the eventual outcome was a compromise solution of sorts. Moreover, even though the Soviets responded to the blockade and did not make their choice of a strategy independently of the American strategy choice, the fact that the United States held out the possibility of escalating the conflict to at least an air strike would seem to indicate that the initial blockade decision was not considered final— that is, the United States considered its strategy choices still open after imposing the blockade.

The game-tree representation of Chicken in chapter 1 (figure 1.4) better models the sequential aspects of Chicken, in which each side permits itself a recourse should the other side fail to cooperate. Yet, such a representation of the Cuban missile crisis seems implausible, for the crisis seems better viewed as a breakdown, albeit temporary, in the deterrence relationship between the superpowers that had persisted from World War II until that point.

To be sure, the Soviets undoubtedly concluded that it was no longer in their interest to sustain this relationship because they calculated that any reprisals for installing the missiles would not be too severe. Presumably, they did not reckon the probability of nuclear war to be high, thereby making it rational for them to risk provoking the United States.

Although this thinking may be more or less correct, there are good reasons for believing that United States policymakers viewed the game as not Chicken at all, at least as far as they ranked the possible outcomes. In figure 2.2, I offer an alternative representation of the Cuban missile crisis,[5] retaining the same strategies for both players as given in the Chicken representation (figure 2.1) but assuming a different ranking of outcomes by the United States (the arrows in this figure will be explained later). These rankings may be interpreted as follows:

1. BW: The choice of blockade by the United States and withdrawal by the Soviet Union remains the compromise outcome for both players—(3,3).

---

5. Still a different 2 × 2 game is proposed in Glenn H. Snyder and Paul Diesing, *Conflict among Nations: Bargaining, Decision Making, and Systems Structure in International Crises* (Princeton, NJ: Princeton University Press, 1977), pp. 114–16; an "improved metagame analysis" of the crisis is presented in Niall M. Fraser and Keith W. Hipel, "Dynamic Modeling of the Cuban Missile Crisis," *Conflict Management and Peace Science* 6, no. 2 (Spring 1982–83):1–18.

FIGURE 2.2   Payoff Matrix of Alternative Representation of the
Cuban Missile Crisis

		Soviet Union	
		Withdrawal (w)	Maintenance (m)
United States	Blockade (b)	(3,3) Compromise ⇑	→ (1,4) Soviet victory, U.S. capitulation ⇓
	Air strike (a)	(2,2) "Dishonorable" U.S. action, Soviets thwarted	← (4,1) "Honorable" U.S. action, Soviets thwarted

Key: (x,y) = (rank of United States, rank of Soviet Union)
4 = best; 3 = next best; 2 = next worst; 1 = worst
Arrows indicate rational moves of United States (vertical) and Soviet Union
(horizontal); double arrows signify moving power of United States (see text)

2. BM: In the face of a U.S. blockade, Soviet maintenance of their missiles leads to a Soviet victory (their best outcome) and U.S. capitulation (their worst outcome)—(1,4).
3. AM: An air strike that destroys the missiles that the Soviets were maintaining is an "honorable" U.S. action (their best outcome) and thwarts the Soviets (their worst outcome)—(4,1).
4. AW: An air strike that destroys the missiles that the Soviets were withdrawing is a "dishonorable" U.S. action (their next-worst outcome) and thwarts the Soviets (their next-worst outcome)—(2,2).

Even though an air strike thwarts the Soviets in the case of both outcomes (2,2) and (4,1), I interpret (2,2) to be a less damaging outcome for the Soviet Union because world opinion, it may be surmised, would condemn the air strike as an "overreaction" if there were clear evidence that the Soviets were in the process of withdrawing their missiles, anyway. On the other hand, given no such evidence, a U.S. air strike, perhaps followed by an invasion, would probably be viewed by U.S. policymakers as a necessary, if not "honorable," action to dislodge the Soviet missiles, whereas an air strike in the face of Soviet

withdrawal would be unnecessary and, consequently, "dishonorable."
[If one did not view AM as the best outcome for the United States, as
indicated in figure 2.2, but instead as the next-best—as (3,1), with the
compromise outcome (4,3) viewed as best—the subsequent analysis of
deception possibilities in this game in section 2.3 would not be affected.]

Before analyzing these possibilities, however, I shall offer a brief
justification—mainly in the words of the participants—for the alternative ranking and interpretation of outcomes. The principal protagonists, of course, were John Kennedy and Nikita Khrushchev, the
leaders of the two countries. Their private communications over the
thirteen days of the crisis indicate that they both understood the dire
consequences of precipitous action and shared, in general terms, a
common interest in preventing nuclear war. For the purpose of the
present analysis, however, what is relevant are their specific preferences for each outcome.

Did the United States prefer an air strike (and possible invasion) to
the blockade (and its eventual removal), given that the Soviets would
withdraw their missiles? In responding to a letter from Khrushchev,
Kennedy said:

If you would agree to remove these weapons systems from Cuba . . . we, on
our part, would agree . . . (a) to remove promptly the quarantine measures now
in effect and (b) to give assurances against an invasion of Cuba.[6]

This statement is consistent with the alternative representation of the
crisis [since (3,3) is preferred to (2,2) by the United States] but not
consistent with the Chicken representation [since (4,2) is preferred to
(3,3) by the United States].

Did the United States prefer an air strike to the blockade, given that
the Soviets would maintain their missiles? According to Robert Kennedy, a close adviser to his brother during the crisis, "If they did not
remove those bases, we would remove them."[7] This statement is consistent with the alternative representation [since (4,1) is preferred to
(1,4) by the United States] but not consistent with the Chicken representation [since (2,4) is preferred to (1,1) by the United States].

6. Allison, *Essence of Decision*, p. 228.
7. Kennedy, *Thirteen Days*, p. 170.

Finally, it is well known that several of President Kennedy's advisers felt very reluctant to initiate an attack against Cuba without exhausting less belligerent courses of action that might bring about removal of the missiles with less risk and greater sensitivity to American ideals and values. As Robert Kennedy put it, an immediate attack would be looked upon as "a Pearl Harbor in reverse, and it would blacken the name of the United States in the pages of history."[8] This statement is consistent with the United States' ranking the outcome AW next worst (2)—a "dishonorable" U.S. action in the figure 2.2 representation—rather than best (4)—a U.S. victory in the figure 2.1 representation of Chicken.

If the figure 2.2 representation of the Cuban missile crisis is a more realistic representation of the participants' perceptions than is the figure 2.1 representation, it still offers little in the way of explanation of how the compromise (3,3) outcome was achieved and rendered stable. After all, as in Chicken, this outcome is not a Nash equilibrium; but unlike in Chicken, no other outcome in the figure 2.2 game is stable either.

The instability of outcomes in this game can be seen most easily by examining the cycle of preferences, indicated by the arrows (ignore for now the distinction between single and double arrows) between all pairs of adjacent outcomes. These arrows show that, at each outcome, one player always has an incentive to move to another outcome—in the same row or column—because it can do better by such a move: the Soviets from (3,3) to (1,4); the United States from (1,4) to (4,1); the Soviets from (4,1) to (2,2); and the United States from (2,2) to (3,3).

Because one player always has an incentive to move from every outcome, none of the outcomes in the figure 2.2 game is a Nash equilibrium, as (4,2) and (2,4) are in Chicken (see section 1.2). Neither does either player have a dominant, or unconditionally best, strategy: as in Chicken, each player's best strategy depends on the strategy choice of the other player. Thus, for example, the United States prefers B if the Soviets choose w, but A if they choose M.

How, then, can one explain the choice of (3,3) in the figure 2.2 game, given this is a plausible reconstruction of the crisis? I shall suggest in section 2.3 two qualitatively different sorts of explanation, one based on deception by the Soviet Union and the other based on the exercise of two different kinds of power by the United States. Then, in

8. Theodore C. Sorensen, *Kennedy* (New York: Harper and Row, 1965), p. 684.

section 2.4, I shall present a game-tree reconstruction of sequential choices in the crisis.

2.3. Deception and Power in the Cuban Missile Crisis

Define a player's *deception strategy* to be a false announcement of his preferences to induce the other player to choose a strategy favorable to the deceiver.[9] For deception to work, the deceived player must (1) not know the deceiver's true preference ranking (otherwise the deceiver's false announcement would not be believed) and (2) not have a dominant strategy (otherwise the deceived would always choose it, whatever the deceiver announced his own preferences to be).

Given that conditions (1) and (2) are met, the deceiver, by announcing one of his two strategies to be dominant, can induce the deceived to believe he will always choose it. Anticipating this choice, the deceived will then be motivated to choose his strategy that leads to the better of his two outcomes associated with the deceiver's (presumed) dominant strategy.

Before illustrating the possible use of deception by the Soviets in the figure 2.2 game, consider the sequence of communications that led to a resolution of the crisis. First, as the crisis heightened, the Soviets indicated an increasing predisposition to withdraw rather than maintain their missiles if the United States would not attack Cuba and pledge not to invade it in the future. In support of this shift in preferences, contrast two statements by Premier Khrushchev, the first in a letter to the British pacifist, Bertrand Russell, the second in a letter to President Kennedy:

If the way to the aggressive policy of the American Government is not blocked, the people of the United States and other nations will have to pay with millions of lives for this policy.[10]

9. Brams, "Deception in 2 × 2 Games"; Steven J. Brams and Frank C. Zagare, "Deception in Simple Voting Games," *Social Science Research* 6 (September 1977):257–72; Frank C. Zagare, "The Geneva Conference of 1954: A Case of Tacit Deception," *International Studies Quarterly* 23, no. 3 (September 1979):390–411; Steven J. Brams and Frank C. Zagare, "Double Deception: Two against One in Three-Person Games," *Theory and Decision* 13, no. 1 (March 1981):81–90; and Douglas Muzzio, *Watergate Games* (New York: New York University Press, 1982), pp. 43–50. A useful compilation of material on deception, both in theory and practice, is Donald C. Daniel and Katherine L. Herbig, eds., *Strategic Military Deception* (New York: Pergamon, 1982).

10. Divine, *Cuban Missile Crisis*, p. 38.

If assurances were given that the President of the United States would not participate in an attack on Cuba and the blockade lifted, then the question of the removal or the destruction of the missile sites in Cuba would then be an entirely different question.[11]

Finally, in an almost complete about-face, Khrushchev, in a second letter to Kennedy, all but reversed his original position and agreed to remove the missiles from Cuba, though he demanded the quid pro quo alluded to earlier (which was ignored by Kennedy in his response, quoted earlier):

We agree to remove those weapons from Cuba which you regard as offensive weapons. . . . The United States, on its part, bearing in mind the anxiety and concern of the Soviet state, will evacuate its analogous weapons from Turkey.[12]

Khrushchev, who had previously warned (in his first letter to Kennedy) that "if people do not show wisdom, then in the final analysis they will come to clash, like blind moles,"[13] seemed, over the course of the crisis, quite ready to soften his original position. This is not to say that his later statements misrepresented his true preferences—on the contrary, his language evoking the fear of nuclear war has the ring of truth to it. Whether he actually changed his preferences or simply retreated strategically from his earlier pronouncements, there was a perceptible shift from a noncooperative position (maintain the missiles regardless) to a conditionally cooperative position (withdraw the missiles if the United States would also cooperate).

Perhaps the most plausible explanation for Khrushchev's modification of his position is that there was, in Howard's phrase, a "deterioration" in his original preferences in the face of their possibly apocalyptic game-theoretic consequences.[14] By interchanging, in effect, 3 and 4 in the Soviet preferences in figure 2.2, Khrushchev made w appear dominant, thereby inducing the United States also to cooperate (choose B). The resulting (3,3) outcome is next best for both players.

Whether Khrushchev deceived Kennedy or actually changed his preferences, the effect is the same in inducing the compromise that was actually selected by both sides. Although there seems to be no evidence

11. Divine, *Cuban Missile Crisis,* p. 47.
12. Divine, *Cuban Missile Crisis,* p. 49.
13. Divine, *Cuban Missile Crisis,* p. 47.
14. Nigel Howard, *Paradoxes of Rationality: Theory of Metagames and Political Behavior* (Cambridge, MA: MIT Press, 1971), pp. 148, 199–201.

that conclusively establishes whether Khrushchev's shift was honest or deceptive, this question is not crucial to the analysis. True, I have developed the analysis in terms of rational deception strategies, but it could as well be interpreted in terms of genuine changes in preferences, given that preferences are not considered immutable.

Could the United States have deceived the Soviets to induce (3,3)? The answer is no: if the United States had made B appear dominant, the Soviets would have chosen M, resulting in (1,4); if the United States had made A appear dominant, the Soviets would have chosen w, resulting in (2,2). Paradoxically, because the United States, as a deceiver, could not ensure an outcome better than its next worst (2)—whatever preferences it announced—it was in *its* interest to be deceived (or at least induced) so (3,3) could be implemented.

More generally, in five of the 78 strictly ordinal 2 × 2 games, at least one player can do better as the deceived than deceiver, so he profits if he does not know the preferences of the other player and the other player knows that he does not know.[15] For this set of games, the odd notion that "ignorance is strength"—or "ignorance is bliss"—seems well founded.

Is there any way that the United States, on its own, could have engineered the (3,3) outcome? One possible means would be to play it safe by choosing its *security-level strategy*. (A player's *security level* is the best outcome or payoff he can ensure for himself, whatever strategy the other player chooses, which in this case is the United States' next-worst outcome of 2.) The choice of such a strategy to avoid its worst outcome (1) means choosing A; if the Soviets also choose their security-level strategy (w), the resulting outcome would be (2,2), which is Pareto-inferior to (3,3) (see section 1.2).

If it is reasonable to assume that, because the conflict occurred in the Caribbean in the U.S. sphere of influence, the United States could exercise greater power than the Soviet Union, then there are means by which the United States can induce (3,3). Indeed, three kinds of power defined for 2 × 2 games—moving, staying, and threat—can all be used to implement (3,3),[16] but here I shall illustrate only the use of moving and threat power. (Staying power will be illustrated in section 2.8.)

15. Brams, "Deception in 2 × 2 Games."

16. Steven J. Brams, *Superior Beings: If They Exist, How Would We Know? Game-Theoretic Implications of Omniscience, Omnipotence, Immortality, and Incomprehensibility* (New York: Springer-Verlag, 1983).

Moving power is the ability of a player to continue moving in a game that cycles, like that in figure 2.2, when the other player must eventually stop.[17] Assume that the United States has moving power, which I indicate by the vertical double arrows in figure 2.2. This means that the United States will be able to hold out longer than the Soviet Union in the move-countermove cycle shown in figure 2.2.

Eventually, then, the Soviet Union must break the cycle when it has the next move—at either (3,3) or (4,1), from which the single arrows emanate. Because the Soviets prefer (3,3), this is the moving-power outcome the United States can eventually implement.

The *threat power* the United States has in the figure 2.2 game is of the deterrent variety:[18] by threatening to choose A, which includes the Soviet Union's two worst outcomes, the United States can induce the Soviets to choose w when the United States chooses B, resulting in (3,3). Even though the Soviets have an incentive to move from (3,3) to (1,4), as indicated by the top horizontal arrow, they would be deterred from doing so by the threat that if they did, the United States would choose its strategy A and stay there, inflicting upon the Soviets an outcome inferior to (3,3)—presumably (2,2), their better outcome in this row. Because it is rational for the Soviets to accede to this threat, given that the United States has threat power, the possession of such power by the United States can also be used to implement (3,3).

It turns out that if the Soviet Union had moving or threat power in the figure 2.2 game, it, too, could implement (3,3). Similarly, the possession of staying power by either player would also lead to the implementation of (3,3).[19]

Because whoever possesses any of the three kinds of power has no effect on the outcome [(3,3)] that would be implemented in the figure

17. Steven J. Brams, "Omniscience and Omnipotence: How They May Help—or Hurt—in a Game," *Inquiry* 25, no. 2 (June 1982):217–31.

18. Steven J. Brams and Marek P. Hessel, "Threat Power in Sequential Games," *International Studies Quarterly* 28, no. 1 (March 1984):15–36. In this article, "deterrent" threats are formally distinguished from "compellent" threats, which is a distinction originally made in Thomas C. Schelling, *Arms and Influence* (New Haven: Yale University Press, 1966). For an illuminating political-strategic analysis of threats, supported by numerous case studies, see James L. Payne, *The American Threat: National Security and Foreign Policy* (College Station, TX: Lytton, 1981).

19. Steven J. Brams and Marek P. Hessel, "Staying Power in 2 × 2 Games," *Theory and Decision* 15, no. 3 (September 1983):279–302.

2.2 game, such power is said to be *ineffective*. However, though ineffective, its impact certainly is salutary in allowing the players to avoid a worse outcome [for example, (2,2)] in a game in which neither player has a dominant strategy, there are no Nash equilibria, and, consequently, there is no indubitably rational choice.

Thus, as with being deceived, being influenced into choosing an outcome in a thoroughly unstable game, like that in figure 2.2, may not be unrewarding. Quite the contrary: one player's ability to deceive (or induce) the other player may be critical in effecting a compromise outcome like (3,3).

2.4. A Sequential View of the Cuban Missile Crisis

Whether any of these forces was instrumental in resolving the Cuban missile crisis is hard to say with certitude. In fact, a much simpler calculation might have been made, as illustrated by the game tree and payoff matrix in figure 2.3. Here I have altered the preferences of the players once again to illustrate another plausible rendering of the alternatives, and the preferences of the players for them, in an extensive-form game.[20]

In the game tree at the top, the United States can choose between a blockade initially and an immediate air strike (the later air-strike option is considered only if the Soviets do not cooperate by maintaining their missiles). If the United States chooses blockade, the Soviets can choose, as before, between maintaining and withdrawing their missiles. Finally, if they choose not to cooperate by maintaining their missiles, then the United States can choose between no escalation by continuing the blockade (blockade subsequently) or escalation (to later air strike), assuming it had previously demurred.

For the preferences shown, which I shall not try to justify here because they are similar (though not identical) to those given for the players earlier, start the backward-induction process (section 1.4) at the bottom of the game tree. The United States would prefer—should play of the game reach this point—air strike to blockade, so cut the latter branch to indicate it will not be chosen and that (3,1) would be the outcome at this point.

20. This game was suggested in a personal communication from Philip D. Straffin, Jr. (1976).

FIGURE 2.3 Game Tree and Payoff Matrix of Sequential Choices in the Cuban Missile Crisis

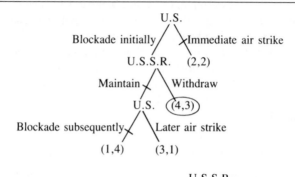

| | U.S.S.R. | |
	Withdraw	Maintain
Immediate air strike	(2,2)	(2,2)
U.S. Blockade subsequently (if U.S.S.R. maintains)	(4,3)	(1,4)
Later air strike (if U.S.S.R. maintains)	(4,3)	(3,1) ← Dominant strategy

Key: (x,y) = (rank of United States, rank of Soviet Union)
4 = best; 3 = next best; 2 = next worst; 1 = worst
Circled outcome in game tree is rational outcome (following path of uncut branches, starting at top); circled matrix outcome is a Nash equilibrium

Comparing, at the next-higher level, (4,3) with (3,1), which I showed in the previous paragraph the United States would choose if it were given the choice at the bottom, the Soviets would prefer (4,3), so cut the "maintain" branch. Finally, at the top of the tree, comparing (4,3)—which would move up, based on the preceding analysis—with (2,2), the United States would prefer (4,3).

To ascertain rational choices of the players, reverse the backward-induction process. Starting at the top of the tree, the players would follow the uncut branches: the United States would blockade initially; and the Soviets would subsequently choose to withdraw. This, of course, is what happened in the crisis.

The normal-form representation of this game tree is shown at the bottom of figure 2.3. Note that the United States has a dominant strategy, but the Soviets do not; anticipating the United States' dominant choice—blockade initially, then air strike if Soviets maintain (indicated by "later air strike" in figure 2.3)—the Soviets would prefer (4,3) to (3,1) and hence would choose to withdraw.

The resulting (4,3) outcome is the same rational choice that was deduced from the previous game-tree analysis (as it should be). The difference is that in the normal or matrix form, strategies describe complete plans of action for all contingencies that may arise, whereas in the extensive or game-tree form only single choices of the players are indicated at each branch.

Whichever representation of the Cuban missile crisis in this and the preceding sections one finds most congenial, together they illuminate different aspects of player choices in the crisis and problems that might have arisen in achieving a rational stable outcome. The compromise reached—if that is what it was—has remained more or less intact for over twenty years, which perhaps testifies to its durability.

Although the United States has had subsequent conflicts with Cuba, none has involved a confrontation with the Soviet Union on nearly the scale that occurred in 1962. As a result of this crisis and the apprehension and fear it evoked, a so-called hot line was established linking the heads of state in Washington, D.C., and Moscow, which has on occasion been used to try to prevent displays of "brinkmanship" from carrying the parties again so close to the threshold of nuclear war.

President Kennedy, at the height of the Cuban missile crisis, estimated the chances of nuclear war to be between one-third and one-half.[21] This estimate is suggestive of probabilistic threats, as developed in the deterrence model of chapter 1. True, Soviet preemption in 1962 involved the attempted installation of nuclear missiles in Cuba, not a threatened first strike with such weapons, but the chapter 1 model, based on Chicken, does not presuppose only confrontations between the superpowers that involve the use of nuclear weapons.

In principle, the probabilistic calculations of this model are applicable to asymmetrical games, such as that in figure 2.2. Assume, for example, that the Soviets threaten the United States that they will

21. Sorensen, *Kennedy*, p. 705.

choose maintenance (with a specified probability) unless the United States chooses blockade. That this threat would fall flat in this game is evident from the fact that AM is the best outcome for the United States.

More efficacious for the Soviets would be what Hessel and I call their "compellent threat" of choosing w and, by not moving from this strategy, inducing the United States to choose B, resulting in (3,3).[22] This is almost tantamount to their deception strategy, discussed in section 2.3, of making w appear dominant and thereby inducing the United States to choose B.

Whether threats are explicit or implicit—as in the figure 2.3 game tree, wherein I assumed the Soviets could anticipate a later air strike unless they responded to the blockade by withdrawing their missiles—they seem to have been part and parcel of the calculations of the protagonists in the Cuban missile crisis. Sorenson described this "game-tree" thinking when he reflected on American deliberations:

> We discussed what the Soviet reaction would be to any possible move by the United States, what our reaction with them would have to be to that Soviet reaction, and so on, trying to follow each of those roads to their ultimate conclusion.[23]

In the next crisis of deterrence that I shall discuss, the hot line was used and probably facilitated the two sides' pulling back from the brink instead of overstepping it. But what has been called for a generation the "delicate balance of terror"[24] surely persists (at least to a degree), and the intellectual challenge of how not to disturb it remains.

2.5. The 1973 Alert Decision

On October 25, 1973, President Richard Nixon ordered United States military forces put on a worldwide "precautionary alert," which is one of only about one-half dozen documented incidents in which the United

22. Brams and Hessel, "Threat Power in Sequential Games."

23. Quoted in Ole R. Holsti, Richard A. Brody, and Robert C. North, "Measuring Affect and Action in International Reaction Models: Empirical Materials from the 1962 Cuban Crisis," *Journal of Peace Research* 1 (1964):188.

24. Albert Wohlstetter, "The Delicate Balance of Terror," *Foreign Affairs* 37 (January 1959): 209–234. However, Intriligator and Brito argue, on the basis of a dynamic model of a missile war from which they derive conditions for stable deterrence, that the chances of the outbreak of war have, paradoxically, been reduced because of the recent

States has employed nuclear threats.[25] This was in response to a veiled threat by the Soviet Union to intervene in the Yom Kippur War that pitted Israel against Egypt and Syria.

Armed with Soviet weapons, Egypt and Syria had launched a coordinated surprise attack against Israel on October 6, during the Jewish religious holiday of Yom Kippur. Although Israel suffered initial losses, a week later she launched a counteroffensive after a promise from the United States of a massive airlift of war matériel.

Egyptian and Syrian forces were quickly thrown back; on October 22, with these forces facing imminent disaster, a cease-fire was called for by the United Nations Security Council. But fighting continued, and Nixon received a note from Soviet Communist Party General Secretary Leonid Brezhnev accusing Israel of flouting the cease-fire arrangement and warning that

if you find it impossible to act together with us in this matter, we should be faced with the necessity urgently to consider the question of taking appropriate steps unilaterally. Israel cannot be allowed to get away with the violations.[26]

Nixon responded by ordering United States forces to be put on a worldwide alert, warned Brezhnev of "incalculable consequences" if the Soviets took unilateral action, but also indicated a willingness to cooperate with the Soviets in promoting peace.[27] In addition, he deliv-

---

U.S.-Soviet quantitative arms race. See Michael D. Intriligator and Dagobert L. Brito, "Can Arms Races Lead to the Outbreak of War?" *Journal of Conflict Resolution* **28,** no. 1 (March 1984):63–84.

25. Barry M. Blechman and Douglas M. Hart, "The Political Utility of Nuclear Weapons: The 1973 Middle East Crisis," *International Security* 7, no. 1 (Summer 1982), p. 132. For an analysis of more than two hundred instances in which the United States used military force to try to achieve political ends since World War II, see Barry M. Blechman and Stephen S. Kaplan, *Force without War: U.S. Armed Forces as a Political Instrument* (Washington, DC: Brookings Institution 1978). A number of detailed case studies of superpower conflict are given in Alexander L. George and Richard Smoke, *Deterrence in American Foreign Policy: Theory and Practice* (New York: Columbia University Press, 1974); and Alexander L. George et al., *Managing U.S.-Soviet Rivalry: Problems of Crisis Prevention* (Boulder, CO: Westview, 1983).

26. *New York Times,* April 10, 1974, p. 9.

27. There seems little doubt that by October 24, when the alert was given, the Soviets were making military preparations to intervene unilaterally on the side of Egypt within twenty-four hours. Blechman and Hart, "The Political Utility of Nuclear Weapons," p. 139; the text of Nixon's message to Brezhnev is given on p. 141.

ered an ultimatum to the Israelis demanding that they permit the Egyptian Third Army, encircled by Israeli forces, to be resupplied with nonmilitary equipment, food, and water.

With the passage of a Security Council resolution on October 25 establishing a UN Emergency Force to enforce the October 22 cease-fire, Nixon rescinded the alert order. The superpower crisis, as well as the prospect of further fighting in the Middle East, abated.

Zagare summarizes the choices facing the superpowers on October 24, and their preferences regarding the consequences of these choices, in the payoff matrix of figure 2.4.[28] The Soviets had to choose between trying to save the vulnerable Egyptian Third Army through diplomatic means or accepting Egyptian President Anwar el-Sadat's invitation to send a military contingent to protect it and the political position of his government. United States policymakers had to decide whether to co-operate with the Soviets to help extricate Sadat from his extremely precarious position or to try to frustrate any Soviet diplomatic or military initiative.

Zagare argues that, with the imposition of the alert, each side's *perceptions* of each other's preferences were as shown in figure 2.4. Had the alert not been called, however, the United States believed that the Soviet perception of this game would have been different. Specifically, the Soviets would have viewed U.S. preferences for outcomes C and D in figure 2.4 to have been reversed: D would have been seen as worst (1) and C next worst (2), as I have indicated by the "interchange without alert" arrow between these two U.S. rankings in figure 2.4.

President Nixon believed the Soviets misperceived U.S. preferences because of the "crisis of confidence" brought on by the Watergate affair. For the alert crisis followed less than a week after the notorious "Saturday Night Massacre," in which Nixon fired the Watergate Special Prosecutor, which immediately led to the resignation of the Attorney General and his deputy in protest. Indeed, some critics of the Administration suggested that "the alert might have been prompted as much perhaps by American domestic requirements as by the real requirements of diplomacy in the Middle East."[29]

28. Frank C. Zagare, "A Game-Theoretic Evaluation of the Cease-Fire Alert Decision of 1973," *Journal of Peace Research* 20, no. 1 (1983):73–86.

29. *New York Times*, October 26, 1973, p. 18. Nixon's concerns about the effects of Watergate on Brezhnev's perceptions are discussed in Douglas Muzzio, *Watergate Games* (New York: New York University Press, 1982), pp. 89, 94.

FIGURE 2.4 Payoff Matrix of Cease-Fire Game

Soviet Union

		Seek diplomatic solution	Intervene in war
United States	Cooperate with Soviet initiative	A. Compromise; Egyptian Third Army resupplied; cease-fire of Oct. 22 re-established; political resolution of Middle East conflict attempted. (3,3)	C. Soviet victory; possible joint Soviet-American peace-keeping force; Soviet military presence in Middle East reintroduced. ①,4
	Frustrate Soviet initiative	B. Israeli victory; possible occupation of Egypt, Syria, Jordan. (4,1)	D. Superpower confrontation. ②,2

Interchange without alert

← Dominant strategy (with alert)

Dominant strategy

Key: (x,y) = (rank of United States, rank of Soviet Union)
4 = best; 3 = next best; 2 = next worst; 1 = worst

Source: Frank C. Zagare, "A Game-Theoretic Evaluation of the Cease-Fire Alert Decision of 1973," *Journal of Peace Research* 20, no. 1 (1983):75 and 77 (figures 1 and 2).

There may be some truth to these charges. The alert seems to have been designed, at least in part, to indicate to the Soviets the U.S. intention of coming to Israel's rescue (outcome D) rather than acquiesce in unilateral Soviet intervention (outcome C). To prevent a misinterpretation of the American position, Nixon claimed that because "words were not making our point, we needed action."[30]

The transformation of the game occasioned by the alert decision has a clear effect on the stability of outcomes. Without the alert, outcome C, perceived by the Soviets as (2,4), is the unique Nash equilibrium. Obviously, they would have no incentive to defect from this outcome, their best; and the United States would have no incentive to move to D, resulting in (1,2), its worst outcome.

With the alert, however, the game would be seen as Prisoners' Dilemma (section 1.2), whose unique Nash equilibrium is outcome D. Since (2,2) is next worst for both players, one might presume that the Prisoners' Dilemma perception on the part of the Soviets would make them somewhat reluctant to choose their strategy of intervention associated with it.

But this strategy is dominant, with or without the alert. In the Soviet view, the only thing that changes with the alert is that the United States would then have a dominant strategy of frustrating the Soviet initiative, leading to Pareto-inferior outcome D.

In fact, however, both sides cooperated in the end, choosing outcome A. How can this action be explained, given that (3,3) in Prisoners' Dilemma is the product of *dominated strategies*—strategies that result in a worse outcome for each player, whatever the choice of the other player—and not a Nash equilibrium?

2.6. Nonmyopic Equilibria and the Theory of Moves: A Digression

From the foregoing analysis, it seems either that the superpowers foresook their rational choices leading to stable outcomes or that these concepts need to be redefined. I shall suggest in this and later sections that the evident rational and stable choices in games like Prisoners'

---

30. Richard M. Nixon, *RN: The Memoirs of Richard Nixon* (New York: Grosset and Dunlap, 1978), p. 938.

Dilemma and Chicken are not so evident if the rules of the game change.

The new rules that I shall introduce in this section allow one to distinguish short-term stable outcomes, or "myopic equilibria," from long-term stable outcomes, or "nonmyopic equilibria." By myopic equilibria, I mean those defined by Nash[31] and described in section 1.2. Nash's concept of equilibrium says, in effect, that a player considers only the *immediate* advantages and disadvantages of switching his strategy. If neither player in a game can gain immediately by a unilateral switch, the resulting outcome is stable, or a Nash equilibrium.

By contrast, Wittman and I, in defining a nonmyopic equilibrium, assume that a player, in deciding whether to depart from an outcome, considers not only the immediate effect of his actions but also the consequences of the other player's probable response, his own counter-response, and so on.[32] I shall refer to this process as *nonmyopic calculation*. When neither player perceives a long-term advantage from departing from an initial outcome, this outcome is called a nonmyopic equilibrium:

The [intuitive] idea is that players look ahead and ascertain where, from any outcome in an outcome matrix, they will end up if they depart from this starting outcome. Comparing the final outcome with the starting outcome, if they are better off at the starting outcome (taking account of their departures, possible responses to their departures, and so on), they will not depart in the first place. In this case, the starting outcome will be an equilibrium in an extended, or nonmyopic, sense.[33]

This new equilibrium concept presupposes a set of rules different from that assumed in classical game theory. Since a *game* is defined to be the sum-total of the rules that describe it, these rules, in fact, define a new game, which I call a "sequential game."[34]

Rule 1, given below, is usually the only rule that the classical theory posits to govern the play of normal-form, or matrix, games. The *theory*

31. John Nash, "Non-cooperative games," *Annals of Mathematics* 54 (1951): 286–95.

32. Steven J. Brams and Donald Wittman, "Nonmyopic Equilibria in 2 × 2 Games," *Conflict Management and Peace Science* 6, no. 1 (Fall 1981):39–62.

33. Brams and Wittman, "Nonmyopic Equilibria in 2 × 2 Games," pp. 42–43.

34. Brams, *Superior Beings,* p. 75.

of moves, on the other hand, postulates three additional rules that define a *sequential game:*[35]

1. Both players simultaneously choose strategies, thereby defining an *initial outcome.*[36]
2. Once at an initial outcome, either player can unilaterally switch his strategy and change that outcome to a subsequent outcome in the row or column in which the initial outcome lies.
3. The second player can respond by unilaterally switching his strategy, thereby moving the game to a new outcome.
4. The alternating responses continue until the player whose turn it is to move next chooses not to switch his strategy. When this happens, the game terminates, and the outcome reached is the *final outcome.*

Note that the sequences of moves and countermoves is *strictly alternating:* first, say, the row player moves, then the column player, and so on, until one stops, at which point the outcome reached is final.

How does a rational player determine whether he should move at a particular stage? I assume he performs a backward-induction analysis, based on the game tree of possible moves that would be set off if he departed from the initial outcome. I shall develop this analysis in terms of row and column as the players, who make choices—according to the theory of moves—based on rules 1–4 and other rules to be discussed later.

In the remainder of this section, I shall illustrate this theory with the game of Chicken (figure 1.1). This is a digression from the previous analysis of the 1973 cease-fire game, but I shall return to this case in section 2.7. The reason for this digression is not only to illustrate the

35. For a full development of this theory, see Brams, *Superior Beings.*

36. By ''strategy'' I mean here a course of action that can lead to any of the outcomes associated with it, depending on the strategy choice of the other player; the strategy choices of both players define an outcome at the intersection of their two strategies. Although the subsequent moves and countermoves of players could also be incorporated into the definition of a strategy—meaning a complete plan of responses by a player to whatever choices the other player makes in the sequential game—this would make the normal (matrix) form for the game unduly complicated and difficult to analyze. Hence, I use ''strategy'' to mean the choices of players that lead to an initial outcome, and ''moves'' and ''countermoves'' to refer to their subsequent sequential choices, as allowed by rules 2–4.

theory of moves but also to show its effects in Chicken, the game underlying the analysis of chapter 1 and also used to model the Cuban missile crisis in section 2.2. The theory's consequences are somewhat different in Prisoners' Dilemma, which I shall pick up again in section 2.7 when I resume the analysis of the 1973 alert decision.

To illustrate the theory, assume that each of the players chooses his compromise c (cooperation) strategy initially in Chicken (figure 1.1), resulting in (3,3). If row departed from this initial outcome and moved the process to (4,2), column could then move it to (1,1), and row could in turn respond by moving it to (2,4). These possible moves, and the corresponding "stay" choices at each node, are illustrated in figure 2.5.

To determine rational choices for the players to make at each node of the game tree, starting at (3,3), it is necessary to work backward up the game tree in figure 2.5, as shown in section 2.4. Consider row's choice at (1,1). Since he prefers (2,4) to (1,1), I indicate "stay" at (1,1) would *not* be chosen by cutting its branch, should the process reach the

FIGURE 2.5   Game Tree of Moves, Starting with Row, from (3,3) in Chicken

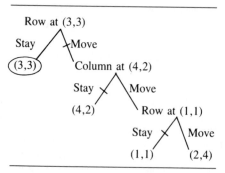

Key: (x,y) = (rank of row, rank of column)
4 = best; 3 = next best; 2 = next worst; 1 = worst
Circled outcome is rational outcome (following path of uncut branches, starting at top)

node at (1,1). Instead, outcome (2,4) would be chosen, which can be mentally substituted for the endpoint, "Row at (1,1)."

Working backward again, compare (4,2) at the "stay" branch with (2,4) at the "move" branch (given the previous substitution). Since column would prefer (2,4), the "stay" branch at this node is cut, and (2,4) moves up to a final comparison with (3,3) at the top node. At this node row would prefer (3,3), so the "move" branch at the top node is cut, and (3,3) is therefore the final outcome that "survives" the cuts.

In other words, there would be no incentive for row, anticipating the rational choices of players at subsequent nodes in the game tree of figure 2.5, to depart from (3,3). Similarly, because of the symmetry of the game, there would be no incentive for column to depart from (3,3) in Chicken. When the final outcome coincides with the initial outcome, as it does in the case of (3,3), it is a *nonmyopic equilibrium*.[37]

For the other three outcomes in Chicken, there is no corresponding incentive for both players to stay at them, should any be the initial outcome of the game. For example, a game-tree analysis, starting at (1,1), reveals that row would have an incentive to depart to (2,4), and column to (4,2). After either departure, the process would terminate because the player with the next move—column at (2,4), row at (4,2)—would obtain his best outcome. But if (2,4) or (4,2) were the initial outcomes, rational departures by row from (2,4) and column from (4,2) would carry the process to (1,1), whence it would go to (4,2) if row departed initially, (2,4) if column departed initially, and stay for the reason just given.

But there is a complication with starting at (1,1). Clearly, row

37. Brams and Wittman, "Nonmyopic Equilibria in 2 × 2 Games"; see also D. Marc Kilgour, "Equilibria for Far-sighted Players," *Theory and Decision* 16, no. 2 (March 1984):135–57; D. Marc Kilgour, "Anticipation and Stability in Two-Person Non-Cooperative Games" (Department of Mathematics, Wilfrid Laurier University [Canada], 1984, mimeographed); and Frank C. Zagare, "Limited Move Equilibria in 2 × 2 Games," *Theory and Decision* 16, no. 1 (January 1984):1–19, for extensions of, and revisions in, the concept of a nonmyopic equilibrium. To ensure that a final outcome is reached, either at the start or before there is cycling back to the initial outcome, the definition of a nonmyopic equilibrium also includes a termination condition, or stopping rule. This condition specifies that if there exists a node in the game tree such that the player with the next move can ensure his best outcome by staying at it, he will. This condition is satisfied by the compromise (3,3) outcome in both Chicken and Prisoners' Dilemma (discussed in section 2.7).

would prefer that column depart first from (1,1), yielding (4,2), and column would prefer that row depart first, yielding (2,4). Since one cannot say a priori which player would be able to hold out longer at (1,1), forcing the other to move first, call the final outcome, starting at (1,1), "(2,4)/(4,2)"—either is possible.

It is easy to show that if (2,4) is the initial outcome, the final outcome according to the game-tree analysis would be (4,2), and (2,4) if (4,2) were the initial outcome. This is because the player obtaining his next-worst outcome (2), by moving the process to outcome (1,1), can force the other player to move to the outcome best for himself [(4,2) for row, (2,4) for column]. In either case, the player obtaining his·best outcome (4) at (2,4) or (4,2) would seem to have no incentive to depart to the inferior outcome, (3,3).

Yet, an objection can be raised to this reasoning: the player who obtains 4 initially, knowing he will be reduced to 2, would have an incentive to move the process to (3,3) first, whereby he obtains his next-best outcome rather than his next-worst. Moreover, once at (3,3), the process would stop there since a subsequent move by, say, row to (4,2) would then move the process to (1,1), and thence to (2,4), which is inferior for row to (3,3).

This countermove to (3,3) by the player obtaining his best outcome at (2,4) or (4,2) would appear to introduce a new kind of rational calculation into the analysis—what the other player will do if one does not seize the initiative. True, I implicitly assumed earlier that each player, separately, would ascertain the final outcome only for himself; yet it seems reasonable that each player would consider not only the consequences of departing from an outcome himself but also the consequences of the other player's departing. Because each player could do better by holding out at, say, (1,1), each presumably would strive to delay his departure, hoping to force the other player to move first.

The situation, starting at (2,4) or (4,2), is the reverse for the players. Although the game-tree analysis shows that, say, row should not move from (4,2) to (3,3), his recognition of the fact that column can move the process to (2,4) would induce him to try to get the jump on column by moving first to (3,3). In contrast, at (1,1) each player has an incentive to hold out rather than scramble to leave the initial outcome first.

In either event, a rational choice is dictated not only by one's own game-tree analysis but by that of the other player as well, which may cause one to override one's own (one-sided) rational choice. Henceforth, I assume that a final outcome reflects the *two-sided* analysis that both players would make of each other's rational choices, in addition to their own.

In the case of outcomes (2,4) and (4,2), it is impossible to say a priori which player would be successful in departing first. Accordingly, as in the case of (1,1), it seems best to indicate a *joint* outcome of "(4,2)/(3,3)" starting from (2,4), and of "(2,4)/(3,3)" starting from (4,2).

In summary, the final outcomes of Chicken, given that the players make rational choices—according to a two-sided game-tree analysis and the four rules specified previously—are as follows for each initial outcome:

Initial Outcome	Final Outcome
(3,3)	(3,3)
(1,1)	(2,4)/(4,2)
(4,2)	(2,4)/(3,3)
(2,4)	(4,2)/(3,3)

If one substitutes the final outcomes for the initial outcomes in the payoff matrix of figure 1.1, the new game shown in figure 2.6 results. The outcomes of this game may be thought of as those that would be obtained if the four rules of sequential play specified earlier, coupled with rational choices based on a two-sided game-tree analysis, were operative.

In the preliminary analysis of this game, assume that each of the two outcomes in the joint pairs is equiprobable.[38] Then, in an expected-value sense, c dominates c̄ for each player. If column, for example, chooses c, (3,3) is better for row than (2,4)/(3,3), which half the time will yield (2,4); if column chooses c̄, (4,2)/(3,3) is better for row than (2,4)/(4,2) because, though the (4,2)s "cancel each other out," (3,3) is preferred to (2,4) half the time.

Strictly speaking, however, for c to dominate c̄ in *every play* of the game, it is necessary to make two assumptions: (1) whenever column chooses c̄, if c̄ for row yields (4,2) as a final outcome, so does c for row;

---

38. The equiprobability assumption is not crucial; it is made to illustrate the calculation of expected values and is contrasted with other assumptions given in the next paragraph.

FIGURE 2.6   Revised Chicken, with
Final Outcomes

		Column	
		C	C̄
Row	C	(3,3)	(4,2)/(3,3)
	C̄	(2,4)/(3,3)	(2,4)/(4,2)

Key: (x,y) = (rank of row, rank of column)
4 = best; 3 = next best; 2 = next
worst; 1 = worst
c = cooperation; c̄ = noncooperation
Circled outcome is a Nash equilibrium

(2) there is some possibility, however small, that the choice of c̄c̄ by the players yields (2,4). In this manner, row's choice of c is always at least as good as, and sometimes better than, choosing c̄.

Assumption (1) above is the crucial assumption. It says, in effect, that whenever column chooses c̄ in the original game of Chicken, and row can hold out longer at (1,1) if he chooses c̄ himself—forcing the final outcome to be (4,2)—row can preempt column at (2,4) if he chooses c, yielding the final outcome (4,2). In other words, if row is the "stronger" player at (1,1), he is also the "quicker" player at (2,4), because he is able to move the process to (1,1) before column moves it to (3,3).

The guarantee of dominance provided by assumptions (1) and (2) seems as plausible as the expected-value assumption, which says, given the equiprobability of the two outcomes in the joint pairs, that c dominates c̄ "on the average." Either way, rational players in Chicken, anticipating the final outcomes shown in figure 2.6, will each choose their dominant strategy c. Thereby the four rules of sequential play specified earlier induce the compromise (3,3) outcome in Chicken, which is circled in figure 2.6.

This, of course, is a rather different argument for the choice of cc in Chicken than the probabilistic-threat argument advanced in chapter 1. In situations of nuclear deterrence, it seems implausible that players would consider actually moving through the $(1,1)$ outcome—though they might threaten to do so—whereas in situations of conventional deterrence such punishing behavior might be considered appropriate to bolster one's reputation for "toughness" and thereby enhance one's future credibility.

As I shall next show, the justification of the $(3,3)$ outcome in Prisoners' Dilemma, according to the theory of moves, relies on different comparisons. The logic underlying this theory seems far more plausible in the case of the alert decision than nuclear confrontations, which are better modeled by Chicken.

2.7. Stability in the Cease-Fire Game

The cease-fire game with the alert in figure 2.4 is a Prisoners' Dilemma, as noted in section 2.4. It is shown as the initial-outcome matrix in figure 2.7, with the game tree of sequential moves from $(3,3)$ shown at the bottom.

An analysis of this game tree demonstrates that, thinking ahead, neither player would be motivated to depart from $(3,3)$, because if he did [say, if row moved to $(4,1)$], the other player (column) would countermove to $(2,2)$, where subsequent moves would terminate.

This is so because if row moved from $(2,2)$ to $(1,4)$, column would stay since by doing so he could implement his best outcome. But since row can anticipate that the process would end up at $(2,2)$, if he departed initially from $(3,3)$, he would have no incentive to depart from $(3,3)$ in the first place. Thereby $(3,3)$ is the rational outcome when Prisoners' Dilemma is played according to the sequential rules.

The two-sided analysis I illustrated in the case of Chicken in section 2.5, when applied to Prisoners' Dilemma, shows that from initial outcomes $(4,1)$ and $(1,4)$ the process would move to final outcome $(3,3)$. At $(4,1)$, for example, it would be in *both* players' interest that row move to $(3,3)$ before column moves to $(2,2)$, where the process would stop, as I indicated in the previous paragraph. Because there is no incentive for row to move to $(1,4)$ or column to move to $(4,1)$ from $(2,2)$, it, like $(3,3)$, is stable in a nonmyopic sense.

Thus, were $(2,2)$ initially chosen by the players, it would be the final outcome, whereas all other outcomes would be transformed into $(3,3)$. Altogether, the final-outcome matrix of Prisoners' Dilemma given in figure 2.7 shows only the upper-left (3,3) Nash equilibrium to be the product of dominant strategy choices by the players and presumably the outcome that would be chosen. Note that it coincides with the (3,3) outcome in the initial-outcome matrix; the other two (3,3) outcomes in the final-outcome matrix are Nash equilibria but not ones associated with the players' dominant strategies.

Thus, as in Chicken, the sequential rules lead to the cooperative (3,3) outcome in Prisoners' Dilemma, but, unlike in Chicken, the implementation of this outcome does not depend on one player's being stronger and quicker than the other. Not only does the dominance of strategies associated with (3,3) in the final-outcome matrix require no

FIGURE 2.7   1973 Cease-Fire Game (with Alert) as Prisoners' Dilemma

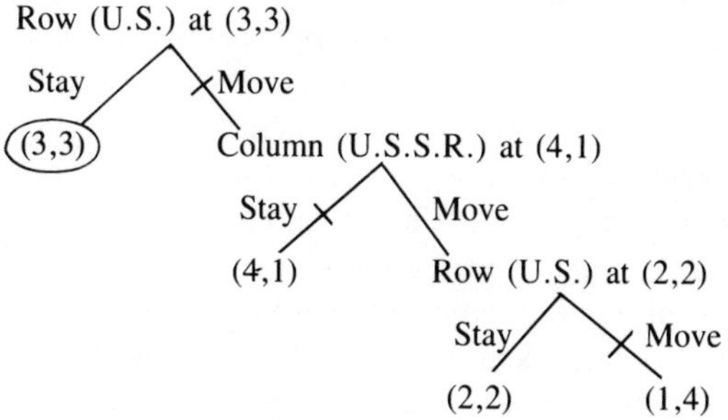

Key: (x,y) = (rank of row, rank of column)
4 = best; 3 = next best; 2 = next worst; 1 = worst
Circled matrix outcomes are dominant-strategy Nash equilibria; circled outcome in game tree is rational outcome (following path of uncut branches, starting at top)

special assumptions, but the dominance of the players' other strategies, associated with (2,2) in the initial-outcome matrix, is reversed.

Thereby, starting at (3,3), it was not advantageous for either player in the cease-fire game, looking ahead, to switch strategies. Had the status quo been the (2,2) outcome, however—as it apparently is in the current superpower arms race (chapter 3)—this outcome, because it is nonmyopically (as well as myopically) stable, would have been difficult to shift from in order to reach the (3,3) compromise outcome.

If President Nixon had *not* ordered the alert, the game would have been as indicated by the interchange of U.S. preferences in figure 2.4. In this game, (3,3) is not a nonmyopic equilibrium, and a full game-tree analysis is not needed to show why.

From the Soviet perspective, if they move to what they perceive to be (2,4), the United States would not move to (1,2). The reason is that if it did, the Soviets would terminate play there, knowing that if they moved to (4,1), the United States, obtaining its best outcome—and inflicting upon them their worst—would stop. [Recall the "stopping rule" mentioned in note 37: a player, such as the United States at (4,1), will always stay at his best outcome if he has the next move.] Knowing, therefore, that the Soviets will not move to (4,1), the United States will not move from (2,4) to (1,2), so (2,4) is the nonmyopic equilibrium in this game without the alert.

As I indicated in section 2.5, this equilibrium is also the Nash equilibrium in this game. Remarkably, of the 37 (out of 78) 2 × 2 strictly ordinal games that have nonmyopic equilibria, only in Chicken and Prisoners' Dilemma are the (3,3) nonmyopic equilibria not also Nash equilibria. This may in part explain why these two notorious games have received so much attention in the game-theory literature. The abiding interest of theorists in them seems to stem from an implicit recognition that mutual cooperation can somehow be justified. But how? Nonmyopic equilibria that allow for the possibility of sequential moves and countermoves in dynamic play offer one justification.

This equilibrium in the cease-fire game *with* the alert would, according to the theory of moves, have robbed the Soviets of an incentive to intervene militarily, whereas the (2,4) nonmyopic equilibrium in the cease-fire game *without* the alert would have encouraged them to intervene. In either case, these equilibria are associated with the U.S. strategy of cooperating with the Soviet initiative.

Thus, what the United States gains with the alert, according to the theory of moves, is not a new rational strategy for itself; rather, the use of the alert introduces a new rational strategy for the Soviets. In imparting nonmyopic stability to (3,3) by stressing its commitment to Israel, the United States makes it rational for the Soviets to seek a diplomatic solution.

This distinction is not made by classical game theory: (3,3) is not a Nash equilibrium in either version of the cease-fire game. The effect of the alert, according to this theory, is to render (2,2) a Nash equilibrium, and the U.S. strategy of frustrating the Soviet initiative a dominant one. Since the United States did not choose this strategy, the applicability of the classical theory is cast in doubt. It seems, instead, that both superpowers acted on the basis of a longer-term dynamic view of the situation.

Whether President Nixon's decision to put U.S. forces on alert status was crucial in preserving the (3,3) status quo is impossible to verify empirically since the situation without the alert never materialized. But the sequential game-theoretic analysis certainly suggests that, at least based on the apparent perception of the crisis by the players, Nixon had good reason to order the alert to deter possible military intervention by the Soviets.

Brezhnev's warning to Nixon quoted in section 2.5 lends credibility, I believe, to this assessment. For had the Soviets sent troops to the Middle East to try to rescue the Egyptian army and save Sadat, and had the United States responded by intervening militarily in support of Israel, the two superpowers would, Nixon believed, have been plunged into an arena with "an extremely dangerous potential for great power rivalry."[39]

The alert may well have averted this situation and the potentially serious risk of nuclear war. Yet, raising the stakes with the alert is what Zagare calls "a very dangerous game indeed."[40] Even Secretary of State Henry Kissinger described it as "deliberate overreaction,"[41]

39. Nixon, *RN*, p. 938.

40. Zagare, "A Game-Theoretic Evaluation of the Cease-Fire Alert Decision of 1973," p. 81.

41. Quoted in Zagare, "A Game-Theoretic Evaluation of the Cease-Fire Alert Decision of 1973," p. 82.

which leads Zagare to consider an alternative game-theoretic formulation that puts the United States in the role of "honest broker."

2.8. Was There an Alternative to the Alert?

Zagare bases his analysis on Glassman's contention that there was a more prudent and less provocative course of action that might also have deterred Soviet intervention:

> Rather than declaring a meaningless alert and putting pressure on Israel, a better response to the Russian threat might have been a diplomatic statement that the United States was also concerned with implementing a cease-fire and that we would seek to convince Israel of the necessity of such a move.[42]

In game-theoretic terms, Glassman's call for an American declaration of its desire to promote compromise (outcome A in figure 2.4, without the alert) rather than an Israeli military victory (outcome B) leads to the cease-fire game, with the United States as honest broker, shown in figure 2.8.

Zagare claims that the preferences depicted for the United States, in which the previous U.S. preferences for B over A are now reversed, were probably true preferences, making its two sets of previously described preferences false and hence deceptive (as possibly the Soviets' were in the Cuban missile crisis, discussed in section 2.3).[43] Yet, if U.S. preferences were perceived as those in figure 2.8 by the Soviets, would the compromise (4,3) outcome in this game have been the rational choice of the two superpowers?

There are sound reasons to think not, despite the fact that this outcome's ranking is raised for the United States, and not lowered for the Soviets, over the previous (3,3) compromise outcome. First, both players have dominant strategies, as shown in figure 2.8, which— unfortunately for the United States—results in the choice of the unique Nash equilibrium, (2,4). This outcome is a clear Soviet victory, best for them but only next worst for the United States. Second, as in the figure

---

42. Jon D. Glassman, *Arms for the Arabs: The Soviet Union and War in the Middle East* (Baltimore: Johns Hopkins University Press, 1975), p. 65.

43. Zagare, "A Game-Theoretic Evaluation of the Cease-Fire Alert Decision of 1973," p. 82.

FIGURE 2.8   Cease-Fire Game, with United States as Honest Broker

	Soviet Union	
	Seek diplomatic solution	Intervene in war
United States Cooperate with Soviet initiative	A. Compromise (4,3)	C. Soviet victory (2,4) ← Dominant strategy
Frustrate Soviet initiative	B. Israeli victory (3,1)	D. Confrontation (1,2)
		Dominant strategy

Key: (x,y) = (rank of United States, rank of Soviet Union)

4 = best; 3 = next best; 2 = next worst; 1 = worst

Arrows indicate rational moves of United States (vertical) and Soviet Union (horizontal)

Circled outcome is a Nash equilibrium

Source: Frank C. Zagare, "A Game-Theoretic Evaluation of the Cease-Fire Alert Decision of 1973," *Journal of Peace Research* 20, no. 1 (1983):82 (figure 5).

2.2 representation of the Cuban missile crisis, preferences cycle, as indicated by the arrows in figure 2.8 emanating from every outcome.

To be sure, the moves from (2,4) to (1,2) by the United States, and from (1,2) to (3,1) by the Soviets, would appear to be irrational switches since they lead to inferior outcomes for the player who changes strategies. However, given that a player who has the next move will stop only if he is at his best outcome (see note 37), I assume these moves would still be made, even though they lead to an immediate disadvantage for the player making them. Ultimately, the player in question, by moving according to the theory of moves, seeks to induce his opponent to countermove to a still better outcome for himself (first-moving player).

This long-term perspective means that the process will never come to rest. The figure 2.8 game, therefore, contains no nonmyopic equilibrium. Nevertheless, outcome (4,3) is an "absorbing outcome," which Hessel and I suggest the players would be expected to converge upon if the possibility of indefinite cycling were precluded.[44]

In fact, the 41 (out of 78) 2 × 2 strictly ordinal games without nonmyopic equilibria all have absorbing outcomes, which are based on less demanding rationality criteria than nonmyopic equilibria. They would seem reasonable solutions to these games if cycling is ruled out as too costly, or otherwise inimical, to the players.

For this reason, Zagare contends that the two superpowers might possibly have settled on the compromise (4,3) outcome in the figure 2.8 game if the Nixon Administration had tried more to promote a policy of détente instead of *Realpolitik* in this crisis.[45] Of course, it is impossible to offer incontrovertible evidence that this would indeed have been the case, though Nixon for one saw "Soviet behavior during the Mideast crisis not as an example of the failure of détente but as an illustration of its limitations—limitations of which I had always been keenly aware."[46] Apparently, he was unwilling to attempt the Glassman strategy, stripped, as it were, of *Realpolitik*.

44. Steven J. Brams and Marek P. Hessel, "Absorbing Outcomes in 2 × 2 Games," *Behavioral Science* 27, no. 4 (October 1982):393–401.

45. Zagare, "A Game-Theoretic Evaluation of the Cease-Fire Alert Decision of 1973," p. 83.

46. Nixon, *RN*, p. 941.

2.9. The Possible Effects of Power in the Cease-Fire Game

There is another perspective one can take, grounded in the theory of moves, in searching for a (hypothetical) solution to the figure 2.8 game. Given that the United States had greater moving, staying, or threat power in this game, it could have used any of these three different kinds of power to implement (4,3).[47]

In section 2.3 I discussed the use of moving and threat power in the figure 2.2 version of the Cuban missile crisis. In the present game, the United States, with moving power, could have forced the Soviets to choose between (4,3) and (1,2), and clearly they would have preferred the former outcome if the United States had shown itself to be (more or less) indefatigable.

Similarly, with threat power, the United States could have threatened the Soviets that unless they chose their first (cooperative) strategy, they (the United States) would choose their second strategy, thereby visiting upon the Soviets their two worst outcomes associated with this strategy. Since (4,3) is better than either of these alternative outcomes for the Soviets (as well as the United States), it would have been rational for them to compromise.

Staying power allows the player who possesses it to hold off making a strategy choice until the player without this power does. Then moves alternate, according to the theory of moves, starting with the player without staying power, with a "rational termination" condition postulated that prevents cycling.[48] This condition specifies that, because the player without staying power does not want the process to return to the initial outcome—from which it will repeat itself—he will act to halt this process before this point is reached.

Assume that the Soviets had chosen their dominant strategy of intervention initially. If the United States had responded with its frustration strategy, resulting in (1,2), rational moves and countermoves would carry the process to (4,3), where it would stay. For if the Soviets moved subsequently to (2,4), the United States would return to (1,2). Because I assume the onus is on the player without staying power to prevent such cycling so the game will be terminated, the Soviets would not have moved from (4,3) if the United States had had such power.

47. Brams, *Superior Beings.*
48. Brams and Hessel, "Staying Power in 2 × 2 Games."

On the other hand, if the Soviets had chosen their cooperative strategy initially, a similar comparison, which can be formalized by analyzing a game tree of possible moves, demonstrates that rational termination would again occur at (4,3). Thus, all three kinds of power induce the most favorable outcome for the United States.

By comparison, if the Soviets possessed greater moving, staying, or threat power, they would have been able to implement (2,4), their best outcome. Thus, lacking a nonmyopic equilibrium, the outcome of this game turns on which player has the greater power (as I have defined these different kinds of power in simple ordinal games).

The figure 2.8 game illustrates the case when power is *effective,* or makes a difference—depending on who possesses it—on what outcome is implemented. Recall from section 2.3 that the exercise of power in the figure 2.2 Cuban missile crisis game was ineffective because, whichever player possessed it, the same (3,3) outcome would have been induced.

The effectiveness of power in the figure 2.8 cease-fire game, with the United States as honest broker, makes the outcome likely to be implemented much more difficult to predict. The player who obtains his best outcome in this game is the player who can continue moving when the other player must eventually stop (moving power), who can delay making an initial choice longer (staying power), or who has the more effective and credible threat (threat power).

Fortunately, perhaps, this game was never played, so the strength of each side was never tested. Instead, because (3,3) is the moving-, staying-, and threat-power outcome in Prisoners' Dilemma—the game created by the alert—whichever player (if any) possesses such power, no test of strength that might have ignited superpower conflict was required.

Games in which power is ineffective probably lend themselves to more amicable resolutions. For this reason, Nixon and Kissinger may be applauded for upping the ante in the cease-fire game, by ordering an alert, so as to generate a Prisoners' Dilemma. But manufacturing a high-stakes game to deter an opponent has its own perils, which certainly must be weighed against the risks of not demonstrating resolve. Zagare offers the following assessment:

It is not surprising, then, that the Nixon Administration decided not to place its faith in détente (or Soviet self-restraint), but instead chose to rely on a strategy rooted in the venerable tradition of Realpolitik, even though this strategy entailed certain risks. Game-theoretically speaking, the Administration's decision was sound and understandable. The long-term stability of the status quo in the game induced by the alert order [figure 2.4] does not depend on either wishful thinking or the benevolence of Soviet leaders, but rather depends upon Soviet recognition of their own interests.[49]

Coincidentally, in an earlier analysis of the 1967 Middle East war, Zagare also found a Prisoners' Dilemma, played between the superpowers over intevention, to have some of the earmarks of their 1973 game.[50] Although there is no indication that the United States tried to misrepresent its preferences to the Soviets, President Lyndon Johnson did put the Strategic Air Command on alert after an Israeli attack on the USS *Liberty,* an American intelligence ship monitoring communications off the Israeli coast that appeared at first to have been attacked by the Soviets. When this turned out not to be the case, the Soviets were quickly informed via the hot line that the alert was no cause for alarm, and the crisis cooled down.

2.10. Conclusions

Because the language of much of this chapter has been about different kinds of equilibria and power, it is fitting—and perhaps a bit eerie—to discover that Nixon echoed these game-theoretic concerns with stability and strength in his own evaluation of the 1973 events in the Middle East: "Any equilibrium—even if only an equilibrium of mutual exhaustion—would make it easier to reach an enforceable settlement."[51] This statement, I think, not only epitomizes Nixon's view of power politics but also is the major theme that emerges from the foregoing game-theoretic analysis of actual crisis behavior.

There are several subthemes worth mentioning, including the importance, but difficulty, of identifying different players' preferences in the real-world games studied. The three different representations given of the Cuban missile crisis, and one (with two hypothetical variations)

49. Zagare, ''A Game-Theoretic Evaluation of the Cease-Fire Alert Decision of 1973,'' p. 83.
50. Frank C. Zagare, ''Nonmyopic Equilibria and the Middle East Crisis of 1967,'' *Conflict Management and Peace Science* 5 (Spring 1981):139–62.
51. Nixon, *RN*, p. 921.

of the 1973 cease-fire game that led to the alert decision, testify to the need to ponder these strategic conflicts from different perspectives that take as much account of the perceptions of players as their true preferences.

In *Rashomon* fashion, each perspective gives new insights. It is especially instructive to see how sensitive rational outcomes are to the different reconstructions on which each is based and the relationship of these to the actual outcome.

A discrepancy between one's preferences and the perception of these by an opponent highlight another subtheme. Lack of complete information in a game may induce one player to try to deceive the other. There is evidence in both of the crises analyzed in this chapter that deception strategies were tried and possibly successful in abetting compromises in each case.

Another subtheme is the need for looking at conflicts as dynamic events that unfold over time. I suggested that the theory of moves, and the nonmyopic equilibria based on this theory, may enable one to uncover stability in certain games that classical game theory hides or places elsewhere.

A subtheme, related to this theory, is the potential importance of power in different games. In political science and international relations, power has proved to be a very elusive concept, even at a theoretical level, but definitions that tap different aspects of power—moving, staying, and threat in this analysis—come to the fore naturally in sequential games in which players can make rational moves and countermoves.

Different constraints on such moves can provide different measures of power. I have not attempted in this chapter to explore the full dimensions of the constraints that one player can impose upon another, for I have dealt with this topic elsewhere.[52] Rather, my purpose here has been to try to give certain strategic insights into the two deterrence crises—both, happily, resolved peacefully between the superpowers—that I think less systematic and formal analysis either does not facilitate or sometimes even permit. As situations become more complex and the feasible options available to decision makers more numerous, the need

52. Brams, *Superior Beings.*

for more systematic analysis becomes greater and offhand calculations more hazardous if a cataclysm is to be avoided.

To return to the Nixon quotation, I think he correctly identifies the importance of "equilibrium" in any enforceable settlement. But what is its basis, and how is it enforced? I believe the theory of moves and its ancillary concepts, whose application to the events of 1962 and 1973 I have tried to illustrate in this chapter, provide some answers.

To act farsightedly, according to this theory, may not be enough, though. A theory that assumes only ordinal preferences, while it allows one to probe deeply into certain strategic structures—played out dynamically—gives short shrift to others.

The probabilistic threats underlying the deterrence strategies of chapter 1, for example, are masked by such a theory. In the next two chapters, I shall reintroduce probabilistic and expected-payoff calculations to try to delve deeper into both the structure of the superpower arms race and possible means to control it, including the verification of arms-control agreements.

3 The Arms Race

3.1. Introduction

The nuclear arms race between the United States and the Soviet Union has proved to be perhaps the most colossally intractable problem of the contemporary world. Its intractability stems not from the awesome amounts both sides have expended on arms, nor from the millions of lives at stake should the arms race culminate in a nuclear war. Although these facts help to explain why the arms race looms so large in our lives, they do not explain why this race has proved so unrelentingly difficult to slow down.[1]

Several hypotheses for the persistence of the arms race have been advanced: (1) the military-industrial complex in each country is said to hold sway over major policy decisions;[2] (2) the economy of the United States, and perhaps that of the Soviet Union, is alleged to require major military expenditures to avoid recessions or even depressions;[3] (3) the

---

1. This chapter is drawn from Steven J. Brams, "Newcomb's Problem and Prisoners' Dilemma," *Journal of Conflict Resolution* 19, no. 4 (December 1975):596–612; and Steven J. Brams, Morton D. Davis, and Philip D. Straffin, Jr., "The Geometry of the Arms Race," *International Studies Quarterly* 23, no. 4 (December 1979):567–88.

2. Carroll W. Pursell, Jr., ed., *The Military-Industrial Complex* (New York: Harper and Row, 1972); Sam C. Sarkesian, ed., *The Millitary-Industrial Complex: A Reassessment* (Beverly Hills, CA: Sage, 1972); and Steven Rosen, ed., *Testing the Theories of the Military-Industrial Complex* (Lexington, MA: Heath, 1973).

3. Kenneth E. Boulding, ed., *Peace and the War Industry* (New Brunswick, NJ: Transaction, 1973); Bernard Udis, ed., *The Economic Consequences of Reduced Military*

dynamic nature of an arms race is thought to require that each side match or exceed the expenditures of the other side;[4] (4) where moves toward disarmament are observed, they are claimed to be no more than an elaborate fraud by which the superpowers deceive the rest of the world so they can maintain their hegemony.[5] Other purported explanations of the arms race could be cited, but it is not my purpose to catalogue or criticize them, though I believe all are open to criticism.[6] For the most part, they are ad hoc, single-factor explanations—sometimes colored by ideological considerations—that are not embedded in a general model that disciplines the weighing of benefits and costs to decision makers in the arms race.

A different kind of explanation of the arms race focuses on the

Spending (Lexington, MA: Heath, 1973); and Wassily W. Leontief and Faye Duchin, *Military Spending: Facts and Figures, Worldwide Implications, and Future Outlook* (New York: Oxford University Press, 1983).

4. Lewis F. Richardson, *Arms and Insecurity: A Mathematical Study of the Causes and Origins of War* (Pittsburgh: Boxwood, 1960); for recent work on "Richardson-type process models," see Dina A. Zinnes and John V. Gillespie, eds., *Mathematical Models in International Relations* (New York: Praeger, 1976); Michael D. Intriligator and Dagobert L. Brito, "Formal Models of Arms Races," *Journal of Peace Science* 2 (Spring 1977):77–96; and John V. Gillespie et al., "An Optimal Control Model of Arms Races," *American Political Science Review* 71, no. 1 (March 1977):226–44. For a critique of the assumptions underlying U.S.-Soviet arms-race models, see Albert Wohlstetter, "Is There a Strategic Arms Race?" *Foreign Policy* 15 (Summer 1974):3–20 and 16 (Fall 1974):48–81, with comments by various people, 82–92; for rebuttals, see Johan J. Holst, "What Is Really Going On?" *Foreign Policy* 19 (Summer 1975): 155–63; and Michael L. Nacht, "The Delicate Balance of Error," *Foreign Policy* 19 (Summer 1975):163–67; for a rejoinder, see Albert Wohlstetter, "Optimal Ways to Confuse Ourselves," *Foreign Policy* 20 (Fall 1975):170–98. A recent assessment of the statistical nature of the superpower arms race is given in Michael Don Ward, "Differential Paths to Parity: A Study of the Contemporary Arms Race," *American Political Science Review* 78, no. 2 (June 1984):297–317.

5. John W. Spanier and Joseph L. Nogee, *The Politics of Disarmament: A Study in Soviet-American Gamesmanship* (New York: Praeger, 1962); and Alva Myrdal, *The Game of Disarmament: How the United States and Russia Run the Arms Race* (New York: Random House, 1976).

6. A recent assessment of different political-economic explanations can be found in Miroslav Nincic, *The Arms Race: The Political Economy of Military Growth* (New York: Praeger, 1982). For a critical review of five recent books on purported explanations of war—not just superpower conflict—see Urs Luterbacher, "Last Words About War?" *Journal of Conflict Resolution* 28, no. 1 (March 1984):165–81.

observation that the benefits and costs to each nation are dependent on what *both* nations do, and hence the arms race may be formulated as a game. The game most frequently proposed as a model of the arms race is Prisoners' Dilemma, which I rejected in chapter 1 as a model of nuclear deterrence but suggested in chapter 2 was probably perceived as the game occasioned by the 1973 alert decision that led to an Arab-Israeli cease-fire.

Of course, any arms-race model that assumes that nations as players have only two strategies, leading to well-defined payoffs, is a drastic oversimplification. However, this simplified model has the advantage that it exhibits, in a strikingly simple way, an explanation of the fundamental intractability of the arms race—based only on the consequences of rational behavior by the participants.[7]

My main concern in this chapter is to investigate a possible solution to the arms race, based on the Prisoners' Dilemma model. For this purpose I posit a sequence of moves by the superpowers that I believe may lay the basis for future cooperation leading to arms-control agreements. (There is already some evidence to support this sequence, as I shall indicate later.) Consequences of this sequence are investigated when each side: (1) possesses an ability to detect what the other side is doing with a specified probability and (2) pursues a tit-for-tat policy of conditional cooperation—cooperation only if it is determined that the other side is cooperating. Given the detection probabilities and the reciprocity norm, I shall show, geometrically, when conditional cooperation between the superpowers is rational and, therefore, likely to occur.

---

7. In a review of several different game-theoretic representations of the arms race, Hardin concludes that Prisoners' Dilemma reflects ''the preference ordering of virtually all articulate policy makers and policy analysts in the United States and presumably also in the Soviet Union.'' Russell Hardin, ''Unilateral Versus Mutual Disarmament,'' *Philosophy & Public Affairs* 12, no. 3 (April 1983):248.

A different approach to rational-choice modeling, using expected-utility models that are not game-theoretic, is developed in Bruce Bueno de Mesquita, *The War Trap* (New Haven: Yale University Press, 1981). Other mathematical models, such as those deriving from Richardson's work, do not share this simplicity, though recent extensions of the Richardson model do incorporate assumptions about goals and their rational pursuit (see n. 4). Also relevant to the questions discussed in this chapter is Martin McGuire, *Secrecy and the Arms Race: A Theory of the Accumulation of Strategic Weapons and How Secrecy Affects It* (Cambridge, MA: Harvard University Press, 1965).

It is important to realize that because this analysis is based on a Prisoners' Dilemma model, it shares the limitations of that model. However, I believe that the probabilistic framework in which the model is embedded, the conditionally cooperative scenario posited, and the qualitative conclusions about the benefits of such conditional cooperation that are derived are realistic enough to throw interesting light on present and possible future developments in the arms race. Indeed, the probabilistic framework imposed on the classic Prisoners' Dilemma game reveals, in my opinion, some consequences of extended play of the game—and, by implication, moves in the arms race—that may bode well for long-run cooperation between the superpowers.

After showing the linkage between Prisoners' Dilemma and the superpower arms race, I shall commence the main analysis by assuming that each player can correctly predict the other's strategy choice with a specified probability. Next I shall show that this model, in which the players are assumed to cooperate conditionally, requires distinguishing a "leader" from a "follower" and is related to the so-called metagame solution to Prisoners' Dilemma.

A new model is then proposed, based on a different scenario, in which the players' roles are symmetrical. In this scenario, I demonstrate when conditional cooperation is advantageous to the players, explore some policy implications of the model, and address some of its limitations. Possible extensions of the probabilistic framework to both new games and different game scenarios are also discussed.

3.2. Cooperation in Prisoners' Dilemma with Mutual Predictability

A symbolic representation of the payoff matrix of Prisoners' Dilemma, analogous to that of Chicken (figure 1.3), is given in figure 3.1, with a game tree shown below the matrix that will be described shortly. In the original story that gives Prisoners' Dilemma its name,[8] two persons suspected of being partners in a crime are arrested and placed in separate cells so that they cannot communicate with each other. Without a

8. See Steven J. Brams, *Game Theory and Politics* (New York: Free Press, 1975); and Steven J. Brams, *Paradoxes in Politics: An Introduction to the Nonobvious in Political Science* (New York: Free Press, 1976).

FIGURE 3.1   Symbolic Representation of Prisoners'
Dilemma as a Model of the Superpower Arms Race

		Column	
		Disarm (D)	Arm (A)
Row	Disarm (D)	(r_3, c_3)*	(r_1, c_4)
	Arm (A)	(r_4, c_1)	(r_2, c_2)*

Row
Disarm   Arm
$E_R(D) = r_3p + r_1(1 - p)$ $E_R(A) = r_4(1 - p) + r_2p$

Key: r_4, c_4 = best payoffs; r_3, c_3 = next-best payoffs; r_2, c_2 =
      next-worst payoffs; r_1, c_1 = worst payoffs
   $E_R(D)$ = expected payoff to row for choosing D
   $E_R(A)$ = expected payoff to row for choosing A
   p = probability that column can correctly detect row's
      strategy choice
   Circled outcome is a Nash equilibrium
   Starred outcomes are nonmyopic equilibria

confession from *at least one* suspect, the district attorney does not have
sufficient evidence to convict them for the crime. To try to extract a
confession, the district attorney tells each suspect the following consequences of their (joint) actions of confessing or not confessing:

1. If one suspect confesses and his partner does not, the one who
   confesses can go free (getting no sentence) for cooperation with
   the state, but the other gets a stiff ten-year sentence—(4,1) and
   (1,4) in the original figure 3.1 payoff matrix.
2. If both suspects confess, both get reduced sentences of five
   years—(2,2) in the figure 3.1 payoff matrix.
3. If both suspects remain silent, both go to prison for one year on a
   lesser charge of carrying a concealed weapon—(3,3) in the
   figure 3.1 payoff matrix.

With this story as background, I shall interpret the game not in terms
of the prisoners' situation but as the situation the superpowers face in
the arms race. In this context, each superpower has a choice of two

strategies, disarm (D) and arm (A), which are analogous to the strategies of not confess and confess, respectively, of the prisoners. The choice of a strategy by each superpower results in outcome (r_i, c_j), as shown in figure 3.1, where the subscripts indicate the rankings of the payoffs by each player.

As a model of the arms race, this game may be interpreted as follows: each player has a dominant strategy of arming, which leads (see section 1.2) to the Pareto-inferior Nash equilibrium, (r_2, c_2). As Garthoff put it, "They [the Soviets] would like to have an edge over us [at (r_2, c_4) if they are column], just as we would like to have an edge over them [at (r_4, c_2) if we are row]."[9] The unfortunate consequence is that both superpowers, by choosing A, are worse off than if they could somehow reach an arms-control agreement and choose D instead, leading to (r_3, c_3). But this outcome is (myopically) unstable—not a Nash equilibrium.

To be sure, it is a nonmyopic equilibrium, as was demonstrated in section 2.7, and the logic of the theory of moves would seem to dictate its choice. But recall that this logic also sustains (r_2, c_2) as a nonmyopic equilibrium. If this latter outcome accurately describes the present state of affairs in the superpower arms race, then the theory of moves offers no panacea for breaking out of it. Only if (r_3, c_3) were presently the status quo—instead of (r_2, c_2)—would the theory support the logic of staying at the cooperative DD outcome in the figure 3.1 matrix.

Is there another kind of logic that offers more hope? The painfully slow progress—and occasional retrogression—that has been made so far in inducing the superpowers to move from (r_2, c_2) to (r_3, c_3) seems to give one little reason to be sanguine.

I believe, nevertheless, that the situation is not hopeless. Because of the recent and substantial growth in the intelligence capabilities of each superpower, which I shall discuss later, each can now make better predictions about the other side's likely choices, using its detection equipment. If each then follows a tit-for-tat policy of cooperating only when it predicts the other side will cooperate, this policy has a surprising consequence for the play of Prisoners' Dilemma: it provides an

9. Raymond L. Garthoff, "The Role of Nuclear Weapons: Soviet Perceptions," in *Nuclear Negotiations: Reassessing Arms Control Goals in U.S.-Soviet Relations*, ed. Alan F. Neidle (Austin, TX: Lyndon B. Johnson School of Public Affairs, 1982), pp. 10–11.

incentive for each player *not* to choose his second dominant strategy of A if each side's predictions are sufficiently good.

True, if one player knows that the other player will almost surely choose his second strategy, then he should also choose his second strategy to insure against receiving his worst payoff (r_1 or c_1). As a consequence of these choices, the noncooperative outcome, (r_2,c_2), will be chosen.

But now assume that one player knows that the other player plans— at least initially—to select his first strategy. Then one would ordinarily say that he should exploit this information and choose his second strategy, thereby realizing his best payoff of r_4 or c_4. But this tactic will not work, given the mutual predictability of choices assumed on the part of both players and the assumption of a tit-for-tat policy of conditional cooperation. For any indications by one player of defecting from his strategy associated with the cooperative but unstable outcome, (r_3,c_3), would almost surely be detected by the other player. The other player then could exact retribution—and at the same time prevent his worst outcome from being chosen—by switching to his own noncooperative strategy. Thus, the mutual predictability of strategy choices, coupled with a policy of conditional cooperation, helps to insure against noncooperative choices by *both* players and stabilize the cooperative outcome in Prisoners' Dilemma.

More formally, assume row contemplates choosing either strategy D or A and knows that column can correctly predict his choice with probability p and incorrectly predict his choice with probability $1 - p$. Similarly, assume that column, facing the choice between strategy D and A, knows that row can correctly predict his choice with probability q and incorrectly predict his choice with probability $1 - q$. Given these probabilities, I shall show that there exists a "choice rule" that *either* player can adopt that will induce the other player to choose his cooperative strategy—based on the expected-payoff criterion—given that the probabilities of correct prediction are sufficiently high.

A *choice rule* is a conditional strategy based on one's prediction of the strategy choice of the other player. In the calculation to be given shortly, I assume that one player adopts a choice rule of *conditional cooperation*: he will cooperate (that is, choose his first strategy) if he predicts that the other player will also cooperate by choosing his first strategy; otherwise, he will choose his second (noncooperative) strategy.

Assume column adopts a choice rule of conditional cooperation. Then if row chooses strategy D, column will correctly predict this choice with probability p and hence will choose strategy D with probability p and strategy A with probability $1 - p$. Thus, given conditional cooperation on the part of column, row's expected payoff from choosing strategy D, $E_R(D)$, will be

$$E_R(D) = r_3 p + r_1(1 - p).$$

Similarly, row's expected payoff from choosing strategy A, $E_R(A)$, will be

$$E_R(A) = r_4(1 - p) + r_2 p.$$

$E_R(D)$ will be greater than $E_R(A)$, making the choice of D rational for row in the game tree in figure 3.1, if

$$r_3 p + r_1(1 - p) > r_4(1 - p) + r_2 p,$$

$$(r_3 - r_2)p > (r_4 - r_1)(1 - p),$$

$$\frac{p}{1 - p} > \frac{r_4 - r_1}{r_3 - r_2}.$$

It is apparent that the last inequality is satisfied, and $E_R(D) > E_R(A)$, whenever p (in comparison to $1 - p$) is sufficiently large, that is, whenever p is sufficiently close to 1. If, for example, row's payoffs are $r_4 = 4$, $r_3 = 3$, $r_2 = 2$, and $r_1 = 1$, then the expected payoff of row's first strategy will be greater than that of his second strategy if

$$\frac{p}{1 - p} > \frac{4 - 1}{3 - 2},$$

or $p > \frac{3}{4}$. That is, by the expected-payoff criterion, row should choose his first (cooperative) strategy if he believes that column can correctly predict his strategy choice with a probability greater than $\frac{3}{4}$, given that column responds in a conditionally cooperative manner to his predictions about row's choices. Note that whatever the payoffs consistent with row's ranking of the four outcomes are, p *must* exceed $\frac{1}{2}$ because $(r_4 - r_1) > (r_3 - r_2)$.

What happens if column adopts a less benevolent choice rule? Assume, for example, that he always chooses strategy A, whatever he predicts about the strategy choice of row. In this case, if row now adopts a conditionally cooperative choice rule, he will choose strategy D with probability $1 - q$ and strategy A with probability q. By the symmetry of the game, if the roles of row and column are reversed, one can show, in a manner analogous to the comparison of the expected payoffs of strategies given previously for row, that $E_C(D) > E_C(A)$ if

$$\frac{q}{1 - q} > \frac{c_4 - c_1}{c_3 - c_2},$$

or whenever q (in comparison to $1 - q$) is sufficiently large, that is, whenever q is sufficiently close to 1. Subject to this condition, therefore, column would *not* be well advised always to choose strategy A if row adopts a conditionally cooperative choice rule. Clearly, if both the previous inequalities are satisfied, row and column each do better choosing their cooperative strategies of D to maximize their expected payoffs, given that each player follows a choice rule of conditional cooperation.

3.3. Linkages to Other Work

So far I have shown that if one player—call him the *leader*—(1) adopts a conditionally cooperative choice rule and (2) can predict the other player's strategy choice with a sufficiently high probability, the other player—call him the *follower*—maximizes his own expected payoff by cooperating also, given that he can detect lies on the part of the leader with sufficiently high probability. Thereby both players ''lock into'' the cooperative outcome, which—it will be remembered—is myopically unstable in Prisoners' Dilemma, wherein the players do not have the ability to predict each other's strategy choices (see section 2.5).[10]

There is one question that remains, however. Given that the follower maximizes his expected payoff by cooperating when the leader adopts a choice rule of conditional cooperation, how does the follower

10. The nonmyopic stability of this outcome, as shown in section 2.7, depends on the players' anticipation of future moves; but here, I assume, the players are only concerned with predicting each other's initial strategy choices and not with subsequent moves from the initial outcome.

know when the leader adopts such a choice rule in the first place? The answer is that he does not (a follower can predict a choice but not a choice rule) unless the leader announces his intention to adopt this choice rule.

To escape the dilemma, therefore, one must assume that there is some communication between the players—specifically, that one player (the leader) announces a choice rule to which the other player (the follower) responds. If neither player takes the initiative, nothing can happen; if both players take the initiative simultaneously and announce the choice rule of conditional cooperation, each presumably will await a commitment from the other before committing himself, and again nothing will happen. Should the players simultaneously announce different choice rules, the resulting inconsistencies may lead to confusion, or possibly an attempt to align the rules or distinguish the roles of leader and follower.[11]

The only clean escape from the dilemma, therefore, occurs when the two players can communicate and take on the distinct roles of leader and follower. Although, strictly speaking, permitting communication turns Prisoners' Dilemma into a game that is no longer wholly non-cooperative, communication alone is not sufficient to resolve the dilemma without mutual predictability. For what is to prevent the leader from lying about his announced intention to cooperate conditionally? And what is to prevent the follower from lying about his announced response to select his cooperative strategy?

The insurance against lies that players have with mutual predictability is that the lies can be detected with probabilities p and q. If these probabilities satisfy the previous inequalities, then it pays for the follower to cooperate in the face of a choice rule of conditional cooperation and for the leader to cooperate by then choosing his cooperative strategy, too. Otherwise, the insurance both players have against lying will not be sufficient to make cooperation worth their while, and they should, instead, choose their noncooperative dominant strategies. I conclude, therefore, that a mutual ability to predict choices on the part of both players offers them a mutual incentive to choose their cooper-

11. The so-called Stackelberg solution in duopoly theory in economics also distinguishes between a "leader" and a "follower." See John M. Henderson and Richard E. Quandt, *Microeconomic Theory: A Mathematical Approach*, 2d ed. (New York: McGraw-Hill, 1971), pp. 229–31.

ative strategies under conditional cooperation. This may in turn inspire trust, for to be trustworthy means, among other things, to be predictable.

It is worth noting that the solution to Prisoners' Dilemma proposed here has some similarities to the solution of this game prescribed by *metagame theory*, but there are also some significant differences.[12] In this theory, the successive iteration of conditional strategies by the players yields some strategies that render the cooperative outcome in equilibrium for the players.

The choice rule of conditional cooperation I have posited assumes, in effect, the existence of a first-level (or "leader") metagame, which gives the follower a motive to cooperate in response to the leader's tit-for-tat conditional strategy. But unlike Howard, I do not carry the analysis to a second-level (or "follower-leader") metagame in which the leader is given a motive to play tit-for-tat against the follower's own tit-for-tat policy, once removed.

The reason I eschew this stepwise backward reasoning is that it seems unnecessary if players' predictions (in the *preplay* leader-follower negotiation phase of the game) precede their choices (in the *play* of the game). Clearly, the proposal of conditional cooperation by the leader in the preplay phase is sufficient to initiate the process of cooperation. Then, however the players become aware of each other's powers of prediction, prediction probabilities that satisfy the previous inequalities are sufficient to protect the players against either's reneging on an agreement. For given that each player knows that the other player's probability of predicting his own strategy choice is sufficiently high, he knows that he probably cannot get away with a sudden switch in his strategy choice in the play of the game, because this move will already have been anticipated with a high probability in the preplay phase. Hence, the assumption that (preplay) predictions precede (play-of-the-game) choices—and both players know this—deters "last-minute" chicanery that would render the cooperative outcome unstable.

12. Nigel Howard, *Paradoxes of Rationality: Theory of Metagames and Political Behavior* (Cambridge MA: MIT Press, 1971). For an overview of this theory, with examples, and some of the controversy it has generated, see Brams, *Paradoxes in Politics,* chaps. 4 and 5. For a refinement of Howard's notion of metarational outcomes, see Niall M. Fraser and Keith W. Hipel, "Solving Complex Conflicts," *IEEE Transactions on Systems, Man, and Cybernetics* SCM-9, no. 12 (December 1979):805–16.

The advantage offered by a leader-follower model that distinguishes unambiguously between the preplay and play phases of a game not only lies in its ability to truncate the iterative calculations of metagame theory; it also offers an advantage in highlighting the circumstances under which players would come to harbor tit-for-tat expectations in the first place. If they come to realize, in the preplay phase of the game, that their later choices in the play of game are, to a sufficiently high degree, predictable, they will be purged of their incentive to violate an agreement, given that they are expected-payoff maximizers.

In this manner, the leader-follower model suggests circumstances under which an *absolutely* enforceable contract will be unnecessary. When the prediction probabilities of the players are sufficiently high (which depends on the payoffs assigned by the players to the outcomes), an agreement to cooperate—reached in leader-follower negotiations in the preplay phase of the game—can be rendered "enforceable enough" so as to create a probabilistic kind of equilibrium that stabilizes the cooperative outcome.

By introducing probabilities of correct prediction *as parameters* in the preplay phase of a game, one is able to place the metagame solution to Prisoners' Dilemma within a rational-choice framework. What emerges as a solution is, in essence, a *consequence* of the rationality assumption (that is, that players maximize their expected payoffs) rather than the *assumption* that there exists some kind of consciousness of predictability among players. This is not to denigrate the metagame solution but rather to show that there is a compelling rationale for its existence within a rational-choice framework.[13]

To what extent do players in real-world political games actually think in the terms I have described? This is a difficult question to answer generally, but one specific illustration of this kind of thinking may persuade the reader that it is certainly not unknown in the field of foreign policy decision making. In describing a highly classified mission, code-named Holystone, which allegedly involved reconnaissance

13. In fairness to Howard, I must add that he argues that metagame equilibrium choices are rational, but in a "stability" rather than an "expected-payoff" sense. Howard, *Paradoxes of Rationality*, pp. 61–63. The introduction of payoffs (and probabilities), I believe, strengthens his rationality argument, though at the admitted cost of complicating his rather spare ordinal-game model—and the theory-of-moves model described in chapter 2.

by U.S. submarines inside Soviet waters, one U.S. government official was quoted as saying:

One of the reasons we can have a SALT [Strategic Arms Limitation Talks] agreement is because we know of what the Soviets are doing, and Holystone is an important part of what we know about the Soviet submarine force.[14]

Almost a decade later, this judgment about the value of submarine reconnaissance as an element of nuclear deterrence had not changed. According to a naval surveillance officer, "We're part of the arms-reduction talks. The Russians have to know that we're good at tracking them."[15]

Before I discuss the role and effects of other kinds of strategic intelligence, I shall extend the probabilistic framework by defining new probabilities, which I call "detection probabilities" to distinguish them from the "prediction probabilities" defined in section 3.2. These will be used in a two-stage model that avoids the leader-follower asymmetry of the previous model but reveals new problems with which players, trying to break out of the noncooperative outcome in Prisoners' Dilemma, must cope.

3.4. Introducing Detection Probabilities

Assume that row (R) and column (C) begin the game by both announcing a tit-for-tat policy of conditional cooperation: "I'll cooperate [that is, choose D] if I detect you will; otherwise, I won't." Then assume both players initially cooperate and choose D, to show their good intentions, though neither player assuredly knows that the other player has made this choice. This is the *first stage* of the game.[16]

14. *New York Times,* May 25, 1975, p. 42.

15. Thomas B. Allen and Norman Polmar, "The Silent Chase: Tracking Soviet Submarines," *New York Times Magazine* (January 1, 1984), p. 14; see also John Tierney, "The Invisible Force," *Science 83* 4, no. 6 (November 1983):68–78.

16. Other scenarios are, of course, possible. But these moves seem the most plausible if both players are seriously interested in slowing down the arms race. Empirical evidence in support of the scenario posited can be found in William A. Gamson and André Modigliani, *Untangling the Cold War: A Strategy for Testing Rival Theories* (Boston: Little, Brown, 1971). Further justification for conditional cooperation is offered in section 3.7, where it is argued that this choice rule's "rationality" depends on maintenance of a second-strike capability that is not compromised by initial cooperation (in the first stage).

The *second stage* begins when each player makes a second strategy choice, depending on what it detected its opponent did in the first stage. Assume that R can detect with a certain probability the strategy choice of C and that C can also detect R's strategy choice with a certain probability. Specifically, let

p_R = probability that R can detect C's strategy choice in the first stage;

p_C = probability that C can detect R's strategy choice in the first stage,

where $0 \le p_R, p_C \le 1$.

Consistent with a policy of conditional cooperation, assume that a player chooses D in the second stage if he detects that his opponent chose D in the first stage; otherwise, he chooses A. Hence, R chooses D with probability p_R, and C chooses D with probability p_C—precisely the probabilities that R and C correctly detect each other's assumed choices of D in the first stage. In this manner, I link the detection probabilities of the players to their (probabilistic) strategy choices in the second stage, though there need be no necessary equivalence; it is an assumption of the model whose implications I shall now explore.[17]

17. Mathematically, this assumption says that the conditional probability that R (C) chooses D, given that it detects the choice of D by C (R), is 1; and that the conditional probability that R (C) chooses A, given that it detects the choice of A by C (R), is 1. In extensive form, each player chooses either D or A in the first stage; then, after detecting one or the other choice (in fact, by assumption, D is always chosen, but this choice will not always be detected), each player chooses D or A in the second stage with expected payoffs to be given. This latter choice, unlike that in the first stage, is not postulated to be either D or A but assumed to be rationally based: D if a player detects D, A if he detects A. The "rationality" of this tit-for-tat policy, however, is what I challenge in this section and—in different form—what I shall challenge again in chapter 4. For a critique of this model, see the comment by Raymond Dacey, "Detection and Disarmament: A Comment on 'The Geometry of the Arms Race,' " *International Studies Quarterly* 23, no. 4 (December 1979):589–98; a response is given in Steven J. Brams, Morton D. Davis, and Philip D. Straffin, Jr., "A Reply to 'Detection and Disarmament,' " pp. 599–600, in the same issue of the journal. Further refinements in this framework can be found in Raymond Dacey, "Detection, Inference and the Arms Race," in *Reason and Decision,* Bowling Green Studies in Applied Philosophy, vol. III–1981, ed. Michael Bradie and Kenneth Sayre (Bowling Green, OH: Applied Philosophy Program, Bowling Green State University, 1982), pp. 87–100. For another critique of the Prisoners' Dilemma model, see R.

Specifically, consider the following question: Does a policy of conditional cooperation benefit the players in the second—and perhaps later—stages of the game?

In the first stage, the expected payoff is r_3 for R and c_3 for C, because, by assumption, the cooperative outcome (r_3,c_3) is chosen with probability 1. In the second stage, the expected payoff for R will be

$$E_R = r_3 p_R p_C + r_4(1 - p_R)p_C + r_1 p_R(1 - p_C) \\ + r_2(1 - p_R)(1 - p_C), \qquad (3.1)$$

assuming R and C make independent strategy choices based solely on their probabilities of detection.

Thus, for example, the first term on the right-hand side of equation (3.1) indicates that R and C will correctly detect their mutual choices of D in the first stage with probability $p_R p_C$: R will detect that C cooperates with probability p_R, and C will detect that R cooperates with probability p_C. If both players follow a policy of conditional cooperation in the second stage, both will choose D with probability $p_R p_C$; hence, R will obtain a payoff of r_3 with probability $p_R p_C$, and C will obtain a payoff of c_3 with this same probability. The probabilities associated with the three other payoffs for R in equation (3.1)—r_4, r_2, and r_1—can be similarly obtained.

Rearranging terms in equation (3.1) yields

$$E_R = p_C[r_3 p_R + r_4(1 - p_R)] + (1 - p_C)[r_1 p_R + \\ r_2(1 - p_R)]. \qquad (3.2)$$

Whatever the value of p_R, the first term in brackets on the right-hand side of equation (3.2) will always be greater than the second term in brackets since $r_3 > r_1$ and $r_4 > r_2$. Therefore, it is in R's interest that p_C be as high as possible (so C will correctly detect cooperation and thereby will also cooperate), as it in C's interest that p_R be as high as possible.

This is not a surprising conclusion. Rearranging terms in equation (3.1) again gives a more curious result:

Harrison Wagner, "The Theory of Games and the Problem of International Cooperation," *American Political Science Review* 77, no. 2 (June 1983):330–46; in response, see comment by Steven J. Brams, Morton D. Davis, and Philip D. Straffin, Jr., *American Political Science Review* 78, no. 2 (June 1984):495.

$$E_R = p_R[r_3 p_C + r_1(1 - p_C)] + (1 - p_R)$$
$$[r_4 p_C + r_2(1 - p_C)]. \tag{3.3}$$

In this case the second term in brackets on the right-hand side of equation (3.3) will always be greater than the first term in brackets, so it is in R's interest that $(1 - p_R)$ be as high as possible, or that p_R be as low as possible. This is because R, if he *incorrectly* detects that C chooses A in the first stage and thereby chooses A himself in the second stage, obtains a higher expected payoff than if he *correctly* detects cooperation on the part of C. In other words, while it is to R's advantage that p_C be high, it is not to his advantage that p_R be high; it is better that he be deceived (that is, incorrectly detect A on the part of C), giving him an "excuse" not to cooperate and thereby realize perhaps his best payoff (if C cooperates).

But surely C could anticipate this unfortunate consequence if he knew p_R were low. Hence, C should not mechanically subscribe to a policy of conditional cooperation in the second stage unless he is assured that R can predict with a high probability his cooperative choice in the first stage and thereby respond accordingly. A similar conclusion applies to C. Within the present framework that allows p_R and p_C to vary independently, this conflict appears irreconcilable. However, by constraining these probabilities in a way to be justified in section 3.5, I shall demonstrate it to be in the interest of R and C that *both* p_R and p_C be as high as possible.

3.5. Equalizing the Detection Probabilities

How can the players' divergent interests in high and low p_R's and p_C's be constrained? One way, which has been proposed in negotiations on a new SALT agreement,[18] is to pool their information so that they both operate from a common (and enlarged) data base. A common data base, presumably, would have the effect of setting the detection probabilities equal to each other, since it would give neither player an advantage in intelligence—assuming no data were surreptitiously withheld by a player. Alternatively, if "national technical means for verification"—

18. *New York Times*, April 27, 1977, p. A7. For an argument that data be collected and verified under UN auspices, see Alva Myrdal, "The International Control of Disarmament," *Scientific American* 231, no. 4 (October 1974):21–33.

in the terminology of current arms-limitation talks—of both players were equally good, their detection probabilities would also be equal.

To investigate the consequences of equal detection probabilities, assume that $p_R = p_C = p$. (This p should not be confused with that defined in the earlier model in section 3.2; in the subsequent analysis, I shall mean by p only the common detection probability in the present model.) The expression for E_R given by equation (3.1) then becomes

$$E_R = r_3p^2 + (r_4 + r_1)(1 - p)p + r_2(1 - p)^2. \tag{3.4}$$

An analogous expression can be obtained for C, but henceforth I shall make calculations only for R since the conclusions derived apply to C as well.

Without loss of generality, assume that the payoffs associated with the best and worst outcomes are 1 and 0 respectively, that is, $r_4 = 1$ and $r_1 = 0$. (This assumption, made for Chicken in chapter 1, simply normalizes the payoffs, fixing upper and lower limits on the intermediate payoffs r_3 and r_2: $0 < r_2 < r_3 < 1$.) Given this assumption, equation (3.4) becomes

$$\begin{aligned} E_R &= r_3 p^2 + (1 - p)p + r_2(1 - p)^2 \\ &= (r_3 + r_2 - 1)p^2 + (1 - 2r_2)p + r_2, \end{aligned} \tag{3.5}$$

which is a parabola in p.

The shape of the parabola in the four regions of the r_3-r_2 coordinate system shown in figure 3.2 is of interest. The parabola tells one how beneficial to R, as measured by E_R, a policy of conditional cooperation is as a function of p, assuming (for now) that r_3 and r_2 are fixed. That is, fixing r_3 and r_2, E_R can be plotted for all possible values of p between 0 and 1; this function assumes different shapes and maximum and minimum values, depending on the region (I, II, III, IV) in which the point (r_3,r_2) falls.

Since by assumption $0 < r_2 < r_3 < 1$, the area on or above the diagonal $r_3 = r_2$ need not be considered. In addition, since the equation of the line dividing regions II and III is $r_3 + r_2 = 1$, the region above this line is defined by the inequality $(r_3 + r_2) > 1$; the region below this line is defined by the inequality $(r_3 + r_2) < 1$. Thus regions I and II are defined by the inequality $(r_3 + r_2 - 1) > 0$; regions III and IV, by the inequality $(r_3 + r_2 - 1) < 0$. It is easy to show that the parabola is concave up (increases to a maximum at an increasing rate) in regions I

FIGURE 3.2   Expected Payoffs in Four Regions

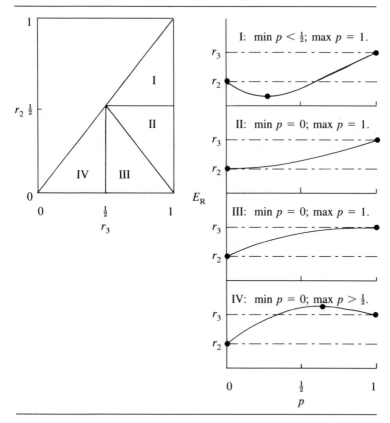

Source: Adapted from Steven J. Brams, Morton D. Davis, and Philip D. Straffin, Jr., ''The Geometry of the Arms Race,'' *International Studies Quarterly* 23, no. 4 (December 1979):577 (figure 2).

and II, concave down (increases to a maximum at a decreasing rate) in regions III and IV (see figure 3.2 for illustrations of these shapes).

In the interval $0 \leq p \leq 1$, graphs of E_R (ordinate) as a function of p (abscissa) are shown in figure 3.2 for each of the four regions. Note that: (1) when $p = 0$, $E_R = r_2$ and (2) when $p = 1$, $E_R = r_3$ in all regions. This can be verified by substituting these values into equation (3.5).

The vertex of the parabola in all regions is at

$$p = \frac{2r_2 - 1}{2(r_3 + r_2 - 1)}$$

$$= \frac{(r_2 - \frac{1}{2})}{(r_2 - \frac{1}{2}) + (r_3 - \frac{1}{2})}. \tag{3.6}$$

When substituted into equation (3.5), the vertex gives the minimum values of E_R in regions I and II and the maximum values of E_R in regions III and IV.[19]

In regions I and II the denominator of the fraction on the right-hand side of equation (3.6) is positive because $(r_3 + r_2) > 1$. Clearly, iff (if and only if) the numerator is also positive will the minimum of E_R be at $p > 0$. This occurs in region I where $r_2 > \frac{1}{2}$. In region II where $r_2 < \frac{1}{2}$, the minimum is at $p < 0$; however, in the interval $0 \le p \le 1$, the minimum of E_R is at the boundary $p = 0$, as shown in figure 3.2.

In regions III and IV, both the numerator and denominator of equation (3.6) are negative, so the maximum is always at $p > 0$. Rewriting equation (3.6),

$$p = 1 - \frac{(r_3 - \frac{1}{2})}{(r_2 - \frac{1}{2}) + (r_3 - \frac{1}{2})}, \tag{3.7}$$

it can be seen that the maximum is at $p < 1$ iff the numerator in the second term on the right-hand side of equation (3.7) is negative. This occurs in region IV where $r_3 < \frac{1}{2}$.[20] In region III where $r_3 > \frac{1}{2}$, the maximum occurs at $p > 1$; however, in the interval $0 \le p \le 1$, the maximum of E_R is at the boundary $p = 1$, as shown in figure 3.2.

3.6. When Is Conditional Cooperation Rational?

The graphs of E_R in figure 3.2 show that $E_R \ge r_2$ for all values of p in regions II, III, and IV; that is, the minimum value E_R can assume is r_2

19. These results can also be found by differentiating E_R with respect to p, setting the derivative equal to zero, and then determining the second-order conditions for a maximum and a minimum.

20. Region IV is the only region in which E_R is not at a maximum when $p = 1$ (in the interval $0 \le p \le 1$). This is because $2r_3 < r_4 + r_1 = 1$ in this region, so that an alternation of the players between strategies associated with outcomes (r_4, c_1) and (r_1, c_4) yields a

(when $p = 0$). Thus, a policy of conditional cooperation that yields E_R ensures at least the security level of R in these regions—the minimum payoff it can ensure for itself is r_2, regardless of what C does. In fact, this policy will always yield an expected payoff greater than the security level r_2 except when $p = 0$, which occurs when R always detects the choice of A by C (the opposite of what C actually does).

No such assurance can be offered to R if it is in region I, where $r_3 > r_2 > \frac{1}{2}$, that is, where both the cooperative payoff r_3 and the non-cooperative payoff r_2 are closer to $r_4 = 1$ than to $r_1 = 0$. In this case, the loss R suffers from being double-crossed is significantly below all its other payoffs. For this reason, it may be advantageous for R to accept existing security level r_2 rather than commit himself to a policy of conditional cooperation. After all, conditional cooperation could result in the payoff $r_1 = 0$, which is much worse than $r_2 > \frac{1}{2}$ in region I.

In region I, the advantage of r_2 over E_R is greatest when E_R is at a minimum, which occurs when $p < \frac{1}{2}$, as shown in figure 3.2. Even for $p \geq \frac{1}{2}$, however, E_R may be less than r_2. To determine how high p must be in order that E_R exceed r_2, set them equal:

$$E_R = (r_3 + r_2 - 1)p^2 + (1 - 2r_2)p + r_2 = r_2; \qquad (3.8)$$

solving for p, one obtains $p = 0$ or

$$p = \frac{(2r_2 - 1)}{(r_3 + r_2 - 1)}. \qquad (3.9)$$

As shown earlier, $E_R > r_2$ if $p > 0$ in regions II, III, and IV. In region I, $E_R > r_2$ if

$$p > \frac{2r_2 - 1}{r_3 + r_2 - 1} = \frac{2(r_2 - \frac{1}{2})}{(r_2 - \frac{1}{2}) + (r_3 - \frac{1}{2})}. \qquad (3.10)$$

Algebraic manipulation gives

$$(r_2 - \tfrac{1}{2}) < \frac{p}{2 - p}(r_3 - \tfrac{1}{2}). \qquad (3.11)$$

---

higher expected payoff than does outcome (r_3, c_3). For this reason, Prisoners' Dilemma is sometimes defined so as to preclude payoffs in region IV. See Anatol Rapoport and Albert Chammah, *Prisoner's Dilemma: A Study in Conflict and Cooperation* (Ann Arbor, MI: University of Michigan Press, 1965), pp. 34–35.

Thus, in region I, a policy of conditional cooperation is better than security level r_2 if the point (r_3, r_2) lies *below* the line, called an *isoline,* which passes through $(\frac{1}{2}, \frac{1}{2})$ and has slope $m = p/(2 - p)$. For several representative values of p between 0 and 1, these isolines—along which $E_R = r_2$ and below which $E_R > r_3$—are illustrated in figure 3.3 and show that as the detection probability approaches 1, the possibility that conditional cooperation yields less than the existing security level vanishes.

Because the slope m of the isolines is convex in p ($d^2m/dp^2 > 0$),

FIGURE 3.3   Isolines below Which $E_R > r_3$ in Region I

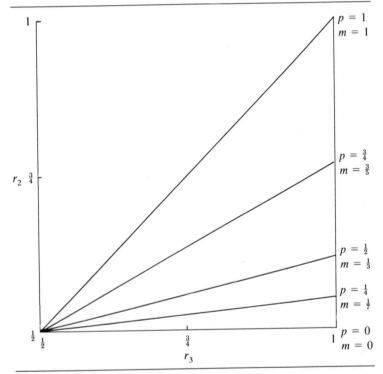

Source: Adapted from Steven J. Brams, Morton D. Davis, and Philip D. Straffin, Jr., "The Geometry of the Arms Race," *International Studies Quarterly* 23, no. 4 (December 1979):580 (figure 3).

raising p will make conditional cooperation more advantageous if p is already high. For example, raising p from $\frac{3}{4}$ to 1 raises m from $\frac{3}{5}$ to 1, or by $\frac{2}{5}$. However, raising p from 0 to $\frac{1}{4}$ only raises m from 0 to $\frac{1}{7}$, or by $\frac{1}{7}$. Since the base of the triangles (that is, the abscissa from $\frac{1}{2}$ to 1) defining the area in which $E_R > r_2$ is the same in each case and the height is a function of m, the percentage of the total area of the large triangle (at $p = m = 1$) that an increment of $\frac{1}{4}$ adds is much greater in the first case (40 percent) than in the second (14 percent). Moreover, since m is always less than 1 except when $p = 1$, raising r_3 [see equation (3.11)] is in general less effective in encouraging conditional cooperation than lowering r_2.

3.7. Policy Implications

I have shown that a policy of conditional cooperation always yields an expected payoff at least equal to and generally greater than the existing security level (when both sides have the same detection probability) in three of the four regions feasible for Prisoners' Dilemma. In these regions, therefore, this policy will generally work to the players' mutual advantage, even if the detection probability is low.

Unfortunately, the arms race between the two superpowers probably occurs in region I. Here the consequence of being double-crossed ($r_1 = 0$) is very unsatisfactory compared with accepting the existing security level ($r_2 > \frac{1}{2}$). Yet the analysis indicates that conditional cooperation even in region I may be beneficial, depending on the detection probability p of both sides. The area in this region, where conditional cooperation leads to a higher expected payoff than the existing security level, increases as p increases; moreover, as r_3 increases or r_2 decreases, the situation is moved rightward and downward, respectively, toward the area where conditional cooperation is advantageous (see figure 3.3). It appears that the effects of an increase in p have already been felt in the limited agreements so far achieved in SALT I and SALT II, although the latter treaty was never ratified.[21]

21. Jan M. Lodal, "Verifying SALT," *Foreign Policy* 24 (Fall 1976):40–64; Herbert Scoville, Jr., "Is Espionage Necessary for Our Society?" *Foreign Affairs* 54 (April 1976):482–95; Alton Frye, "Strategic Restraint: Mutual and Assured," *Foreign Policy* 27 (Summer 1977):3–24; and Stockholm International Peace Research Institute, *Strategic Disarmament, Verification, and National Security* (New York: Crane, Russak, 1977).

If p continues to increase as technology improves, conditional co-operation should become even more attractive. This is because the slope m increases faster than p when $dm/dp > 1$, or

$$\frac{2}{(2 - p)^2} > 1,$$

$$p > 2 - \sqrt{2} \approx 0.586. \qquad (3.12)$$

Thus, technological improvements that raise p above 0.586 will even more rapidly expand the area in which conditional cooperation is rational for both sides.

I indicated in section 3.6 that the effects of a decrease in r_2 in encouraging conditional cooperation are greater than the effects of an increase in r_3. This means that developments that increase the costs of a continuing arms race (decrease r_2) do more to encourage conditional cooperation than developments that increase the benefits of an arms-control agreement (increase r_3).

Of course, raising the benefits of an agreement and raising the costs of no agreement are two sides of the same coin. But if there is a lesson to be derived from the model, it is that the two policies have unequal trade-offs. Since the multiplier effect is on the cost side of the equation, behavior that raises the costs of an arms race provides the greater incentive for making reciprocal concessions.

Probably the best way to make an arms race more costly (decrease r_2) is to invest heavily in research and development. (I assume that such an investment may also decrease r_3 by making the benefits of coopera-tion more expensive to achieve, but it would have a greater depressing effect on r_2 and thus not reverse $r_3 > r_2$ in Prisoners' Dilemma.) This investment increases the probability of technological breakthroughs that create the need for expensive new weapons systems. Paradoxically, perhaps, by making *present* weapons systems more vulnerable to tech-nological breakthroughs, and hence less cost effective, a *future* policy conducive to arms-control agreements may be fostered.

Since the early 1960s, one of the most significant qualitative changes in the nuclear arms race has been the dramatic rise in the detection capabilities of both sides, which has been principally due to the use of reconnaissance satellites.[22] Indeed, President Lyndon John-

22. Frederick A. Long, "Arms Control from the Perspective of the Nineteen-Seven-ties," in *Arms, Defense Policy, and Arms Control*, ed. Frederick A. Long et al. (New

son stated that space reconnaissance had saved enough in military expenditures to pay for the entire military and space programs.[23] President Jimmy Carter, in the first public acknowledgment of photo reconnaissance satellites, said that "in the monitoring of arms control agreements they make an immense contribution to the security of all nations."[24]

If the detection capability of either side is destroyed or even threatened, then conditional cooperation in region I will again be rendered unappealing and the prospects of a continuing arms race will be high. On the other hand, if each side's detection capabilities can be ensured or even strengthened—especially through the sharing of data that helps render $p_R = p_C = p$—then further agreements in SALT (or START) would appear not only desirable but also rational for both sides.

Stability in the superpower arms race has been based on a policy of deterrence or MAD—the ability and willingness of each side to respond to a possible first strike by the other side—as discussed in chapter 1. But if MAD has prevented war, it has not led to a significant *diminution* in the arms race, which now seems to depend on the ability of each side to detect cooperation on the part of the other side and to respond to it in kind. Unfortunately, "probably nothing the United States does is more closely held than the techniques and performance of its verification machinery."[25] To promote movement toward an arms-control agree-

---

York: Norton, 1975), pp. 1–13; Ted Greenwood, "Reconnaissance and Arms Control," *Scientific American* 228, no. 2 (February 1973):14–25; Stockholm International Peace Research Institute, *Strategic Disarmament, Verification, and National Security;* Les Aspin, "The Verification of the SALT II Agreement," *Scientific American* 240, no. 2 (February 1979):38–45; Lynn R. Sykes and Jack Evernden, "The Verification of a Comprehensive Nuclear Test Ban," *Scientific American* 236, no. 4 (October 1982):47–55; and Stephen M. Meyer, "Verification and Risk in Arms Control," *International Security* 8, no. 4 (Spring 1984):111–126. For a history of aerial reconnaissance programs since the early 1950s, see Herbert F. York and G. Allen Greb, "Strategic Reconnaissance," *Bulletin of Atomic Scientists* (April 1977):33–42; and Jeffrey T. Richelson, "The Keyhole Satellite Program," *Journal of Strategic Studies* 7, no. 2 (June 1984):212–53; see also Gerald M. Steinberg, *Satellite Reconnaissance: The Role of Informal Bargaining* (New York: Praeger, 1983).

23. W. F. Biddle, *Weapons, Technology, and Arms Control* (New York: Praeger, 1972), p. 252.

24. *Chicago Tribune*, October 2, 1978, p. 2.

25. John Newhouse, *Cold Dawn: The Story of SALT* (New York: Holt, Rinehart and Winston, 1973), p. 14; security aspects of reconnaissance programs are discussed in

ment, it would seem generally in the interest of both the United States and the Soviet Union not only to improve their own detection capabilities but also to abet the detection capabilities of each other.[26]

Naturally one cannot argue as a blanket prescription that all reconnaissance information about weapons systems should be shared. Information that would greatly increase a country's vulnerability to attack may itself create instability by making a preemptive strike more attractive.[27] Thus, the gains from increasing the likelihood of successful mutual disarmament that both superpowers would obtain through a sharing of information that enhances their common detection probability p must be balanced against the possibility that such shared information could increase their vulnerability to a first nuclear strike. Success, it seems, is never unalloyed.

Since I have precluded noncooperation by either superpower in the first stage of the two-stage model, the incentive to strike first is presumed not to exist. Should this incentive exist, however, it would create a fundamental instability that would render the assumed game scenario implausible.

At this time both superpowers possess substantial second-strike capabilities, stemming principally from the relative invulnerability of their submarine-launched nuclear missiles. Hence, both superpowers have an incentive not to launch first strikes, but instead to find some reasonably safe way to move away from a constant repetition of the burdensome (r_2, c_2) outcome. The two-stage model suggests one way this process may be initiated.

It is important to point out factors that may complicate the rational calculations I have postulated based on the expected-payoff criterion.

Greenwood, "Reconnaissance and Arms Control"; York and Greb, "Strategic Reconnaissance"; and Meyer, "Verification and Risk in Arms Control."

26. Cooperation between the superpowers may also work to their advantage with respect to third parties. When the Soviet Union alerted the United States to possible preparations by South Africa for a nuclear test in August 1977, both countries allegedly worked together to exert political pressure that apparently forestalled the test. *New York Times*, August 28, 1977, p. 1.

27. Schelling makes this point with respect to commitments that, though rational in indicating firmness, may convey useful information to an adversary about details of one's position. Thomas C. Schelling, *The Strategy of Conflict* (Cambridge, MA: Harvard University Press, 1960), p. 176.

First, the concept of "expected payoff" makes most sense when the arms race is viewed not as a one-shot affair but as a multistage game played out in an uncertain environment. Even viewed in these terms, however, there are many possible scenarios, and the consequences of only one have been investigated. It would be useful to investigate other plausible scenarios—perhaps those occurring over more than two stages, possibly with allowance made for the discounting of payoffs in later stages[28]—to determine the conditions that make mutual cooperation rational.

It would also be useful to investigate how these conditions change when the game being played is different. I have in fact made this calculation for Chicken and found that the area in which $E_R > r_2$ is˙

1. larger for Chicken if $p > \frac{1}{2}$;
2. larger for Prisoners' Dilemma if $p < \frac{1}{2}$;
3. the same for both games if $p = \frac{1}{2}$.

Moreover, while for any p in Prisoners' Dilemma, $E_R \geq r_2$ in regions II, III, and IV of figure 3.2, this is true in Chicken only for $p \geq \frac{1}{2}$. Hence, the policy of conditional cooperation is more advantageous to the players in Prisoners' Dilemma for low p, in Chicken for high p.

I interpret this to mean that if both sides are willing to reciprocate cooperative strategy choices in confrontation situations modeled by Chicken, they can benefit even more from good detection capabilities—that confirm this cooperative behavior—than they can in arms races modeled by Prisoners' Dilemma. Intuitively, because the stakes are higher in Chicken, in which mutual noncooperation is disastrous, the players do relatively better when they are successful in avoiding this outcome and achieving (r_3, c_3) instead.

Another way the analysis might be refined, and perhaps rendered more realistic, is to distinguish so-called type-1 and type-2 errors. In the two-stage model, a type-1 error would refer to an incorrect detection of a violation of conditional cooperation when there actually was adherence by the other side; a type-2 error would refer to an incorrect detection of adherence to this policy when there actually was a violation by the other side in the second stage of the game scenario. In a real arms

---

28. Michael Taylor, *Anarchy and Cooperation* (London: Wiley Ltd, 1976); the discount rate is related to the termination probability in Stephen J. Majeski, "Arms Races as Iterated Prisoner's Dilemmas," *Mathematical Social Sciences* (forthcoming).

race, there would surely be different reactive strategies associated with each type of error—presumably a type-2 error would not cause a change in policy, whereas a type-1 error would—and generally different probabilities as well.

Considerable work remains to be done to incorporate these and other factors into the present model. Nevertheless, this model as so far developed offers a way of thinking about arms races as multistage (versus one-stage) games that capture interdependencies over time not heretofore modeled.

Naturally, I do not mean to imply that Soviet and American decision makers should follow precisely the calculations set forth herein. Rather, I believe the model may help them better understand the effects of a choice rule like conditional cooperation in an arms race that presumes similar detection capabilities on the part of the two players.

If the arms race can be modeled by an extended form of Prisoners' Dilemma, there may well be benefits to the two sides' committing themselves to a policy of tit-for-tat under certain conditions.[29] In the concluding section I shall review these conditions and make some more general observations as well.

3.8. Conclusions

I have in this chapter conceptualized the arms race between the superpowers as a Prisoners' Dilemma, with the additional property that each player can predict or detect cooperation or noncooperation on the part of

---

29. This view is supported by a very different game-theoretic model in Robert Axelrod, *The Evolution of Cooperation* (New York: Basic, 1984). Axelrod found that when many computer programs giving strategies were matched against each other in computer tournament play of Prisoners' Dilemma, "tit-for-tat" did better than any other program. That is, if one starts out by cooperating, but retaliates on the next round with noncooperation if the other player does not cooperate initially—and imitates his previous-round behavior in all subsequent play—then one does better on average than never cooperating or choosing most other strategies. (However, there is no strategy that is unequivocally best in tournament play—it depends on one's opponents' strategies.) Generally speaking, it pays to be "nice" (begin by cooperating), "provocable" (be ready to retaliate quickly if provoked), and "forgiving" (by returning to cooperating, after retaliating, as soon as the other player does). These conclusions, it should be emphasized, follow from a model that assumes repeated play against different (randomly chosen) opponents, which is hardly descriptive of superpower conflict that involves one continuing opponent.

the other player with a specified probability. The first model required that one player (the leader) take the initiative and propose to the other player (the follower) a choice rule of conditional cooperation. It did not, however, require a binding and enforceable contract between the two players, which some analysts have argued is the only way to ensure cooperation in this melancholy game. Nor did it require that the players rely solely on good will and mutual trust to bring about the cooperative outcome. Instead, the analysis suggested that there is a third (middle?) road to cooperation—mutual predictability of choices—that renders the cooperative strategies less risky for both players.

If such predictability obtains, then a contract is unnecessary, for violations will be predictable with a high probability in the preplay phase of the game and appropriate sanctions can be applied to the violator in the play of the game. But because such retribution works to the disadvantage of both players, the ability of both players to predict each other's choices serves also to reinforce trustworthy behavior, which is exactly what is not encouraged in Prisoners' Dilemma without mutual predictability.

I showed that this resolution of Prisoners' Dilemma bears some resemblance to the metagame solution to this game, but offers, in addition, a model that rationalizes its existence in terms of the expected-payoff calculations of players. This has the advantage of placing the metagame solution within a probabilistic, rational-choice framework.

In the second model, consequences of the following scenario were investigated: both players cooperate initially; each player, knowing the other player's detection probability, follows a policy of conditional cooperation. Although the players would not be motivated to cooperate, even conditionally, when the detection probabilities are not equal, when they are equal several conclusions follow:

1. Each player's expected payoff as a function of the detection probability is a parabola, which may assume four different forms depending on the payoff each player assigns to the cooperative versus noncooperative outcomes in Prisoners' Dilemma.
2. The different assignments of payoffs can be represented geometrically by four different regions; in only one of the four regions does conditional cooperation not guarantee a player at least the existing security level.

3. Even in this region, as the detection probability approaches one,
the possibility that conditional cooperation yields less than the
existing security level vanishes.

Policy implications of this analysis for SALT were discussed, and a
suggestion for the sharing of intelligence data was advanced. It was
qualified, however, by noting that enhanced detection capabilities may
increase the vulnerability of a country's defenses to a preemptive strike
and thereby render a delicate situation even more fragile.

More attention needs to be paid to the trade-off between the stability
induced by better detection capabilities (increasing p) and the instability
induced by making a preemptive strike more attractive (rendering the
scenario posited implausible). The model indicates that if there is a
choice between making cooperation more attractive (raising r_3) and
making noncooperation less attractive by an equal amount (lowering
r_2), the latter alternative is generally more efficacious in encouraging
conditional cooperation. It perhaps can be best pursued through support
of research that renders weapons systems obsolete as rapidly as possible
and thereby discourages massive investments in them.

I believe the kind of mutual predictability/detectability assumed in
the models has given impetus to negotiations between the superpowers
in SALT and other forums that has laid the groundwork for certain arms-
limitation agreements since the Limited Nuclear Test Ban treaty was
ratified in 1963.[30] With each superpower's reconnaissance satellites
and other means of intelligence able to detect substantial violations

30. Here is a list of the subsequent multilateral treaties:

1967: Treaty on Principles Governing the Activities of States in the Exploration and Use
of Outer Space, Including the Moon and Other Celestial Bodies (treaty prohibiting
nuclear weapons in outer space)
1967: Treaty for the Prohibition of Nuclear Weapons in Latin America
1968: Treaty on the Non-Proliferation of Nuclear Weapons
1971: Treaty on the Prohibition of the Emplacement of Nuclear Weapons and Other
Weapons of Mass Destruction on the Seabed and the Ocean Floor and in the
Subsoil Thereof
1972: Convention on the Prohibition of the Development, Production and Stockpiling of
Bacteriological (Biological) and Toxin Weapons and on Their Destruction
1977: Convention on the Prohibition of Military or Any Other Hostile Use of Environmental Modification Techniques
1980: Convention on Prohibitions and Restrictions on the Use of Certain Conventional

quickly, the abrogation of an agreement by one party will be known before its consequences prove disastrous to the other party and prevent it from taking appropriate countermeasures. With little to be gained from such a violation and perhaps much to be lost, it is less likely to occur.

More positively, each side may even have an incentive to support concrete arms-control measures, not just offer moral exhortations that it is peace-loving. In this manner, space-age technology will, one hopes, stimulate and foster arms-control agreements that—because of the ease with which violations could previously be kept secret—have been so prodigiously difficult to obtain in the past.[31]

I noted that the methodology developed in this chapter could be applied to Chicken, which was analyzed extensively, using different models, in the two previous chapters. Still other games mirror different aspects of superpower confict, and I shall analyze one in considerable detail in chapter 4.

This game will illuminate certain features of the so-called verification problem, which has been implicit in much of the prediction/detection analysis of this chapter. Again, I shall consider possible advantages and disadvantages of tit-for-tat—developed within a probabilistic framework—and other policies as well.

Weapons Which May Be Deemed to Be Excessively Injurious or to Have Indiscriminate Effects

These do not include thirteen bilateral American-Soviet treaties and agreements concluded since 1963, the most important of which are the SALT I ABM Treaty (1972) and Interim Offensive Arms Agreement (1972). Several significant treaties were never ratified, including the Threshold Underground Nuclear Weapon Tests Treaty (1974), the Peaceful Underground Nuclear Explosions Treaty (1976), and the SALT II Offensive Arms Limitation Treaty (1979). For a complete listing and discussion of these treaties and agreements, see William Epstein, "The Role of the Public in the Decisionmaking Process for Arms Limitation," in *Decisionmaking for Arms Limitation: Assessments and Prospects,* ed. Hans Guenter Brauch and Duncan L. Clarke (Cambridge, MA: Ballinger, 1983), pp. 277–93.

31. President Ronald Reagan's "star wars" defense, however, involves a much more controversial use of space than for reconnaissance purposes alone. See Ben Bova, *Assured Survival: Putting the Star Wars Defense in Perspective.* (Boston: Houghton Mifflin, 1984); and Hans A. Bethe, Richard L. Garwin, and Henry W. Kendall, "Spaced-Based Ballistic Missile Defense," *Scientific American* 251, no. 4 (October 1984): 37–47.

4 Verification

4.1. Introduction

"Verification: The Critical Element in Arms Control," the title of a U.S. Arms Control and Disarmament Agency publication,[1] clearly underscores the overriding significance that each superpower attaches to its ability to verify that the provisions of an arms-control agreement are adhered to by the other superpower. Indeed, the two superpowers spend billions of dollars annually to conduct reconnaissance and otherwise monitor the communications and physical moves of each other, as noted in chapter 3. These expenditures indicate the paramount importance for each of ascertaining what the other side is doing and checking this observed behavior against statements of the other side about its actions.

The so-called verification problem in arms control concerns the impediments that may undermine one's ability to determine compliance with arms-control treaty provisions[2] and the correspondence between

1. U.S. Arms Control and Disarmament Agency, "Verification: The Critical Element in Arms Control" (Washington, DC: U.S. Arms Control and Disarmament Agency, 1976). This chapter is drawn from Steven J. Brams and Morton D. Davis, "The Verification Problem in Arms Control: A Game-Theoretic Analysis" (Economic Research Report no. 83-12, C. V. Starr Center for Applied Economics, New York University, October 1983).

2. Stephen M. Meyer, "Verification and Risk in Arms Control," *International Security* 8, no. 4 (Spring 1984):111–26.

statements and observed actions of the other side. Its solution lies in formulating strategies that enable each side to ensure that it makes optimal use of its monitoring capabilities in the face of these impediments. There is a large literature, most of it descriptive, on obstacles that may arise, but little rigorous analysis has been devoted to possible solutions, other than to calculate certain physical effects (for example, of cloud cover) on one's ability to detect certain kinds of military-related activities of the other side.

By "solution" I do not mean specific safeguards one might take against being deceived; these are well described with respect to different weapon systems and the military-strategic doctrines of the two superpowers in several articles in a volume edited by Potter,[3] among other places. Rather, I mean general principles for dealing with problems of detecting the truth, based on an analysis of optimal strategies in games wherein the truth may be fugitive.

To try to elucidate these principles and highlight the theoretical issues they raise, I shall model the verification problem by a simple two-person, nonconstant-sum game of imperfect information played between a "signaler" and a "detector." The signaler can either tell the truth or lie, and the detector can ascertain, with a specified probability, the strategy choice of the signaler and, on this basis, choose to believe or not believe the choice he detects.

If the signaler wants to hide the truth and the detector wants to discover it, sometimes, paradoxically, *both* the detector and the signaler can do better when the detector completely ignores, rather than relies on, his detection equipment. In general, however, the detector should pay *selective attention* to the signal he detects to maximize his expected payoff by (1) inducing the signaler to be truthful or (2) guaranteeing himself an expected payoff whatever the signaler does (tells the truth or lies).

Whether the detector chooses an optimal "inducement" or "guarantee" strategy, it will always be mixed (randomized) if his detection equipment is not perfect. Similarly, the signaler has his choice of these two qualitatively different strategies to (1) induce the detector to believe his signal or (2) guarantee himself an expected payoff whatever the detector does (believes or does not believe).

3. William C. Potter, ed., *Verification and SALT: The Challenge of Strategic Deception* (Boulder, CO: Westview, 1980).

The fact that, under *all* circumstances, the optimal inducement and guarantee strategies of both the signaler and detector are mixed when the detector's detection equipment is not perfect might appear surprising for two reasons, one theoretical and one substantive: (1) theoretically, in two-person, nonconstant-sum games—at least those without detection probabilities or in which probabilistic threats are invoked (chapter 1)—wherein the two players cannot ensure a (common) value (as in constant-sum games), mixed strategies have not been considered optimal; and (2) substantively, the idea of ignoring one's detection equipment, even when its reliability is high, seems to violate common sense.

But perhaps, on this second point, this argument is really no more than an elaboration and formalization of the well-known strategic principle that one should keep one's opponent guessing, making him uncertain of what one's choice may be in a possible conflict by "leaving something to chance"[4] or creating "strategic uncertainty,"[5] as argued in chapter 1. What the present formalization provides in addition, I believe, is a rigorous demonstration that this confusion principle is sound, even when there is rather reliable detection equipment that enables both players to calculate the expected risks to themselves.

That these calculations, and the resulting maximization strategies they imply, may lead to mutual benefits to the players in the nonconstant-sum game posited—or at least provide guarantees of the expected payoffs they can ensure for themselves—offers, I think, a compelling justification that these particular mixed strategies are indeed "optimal." It needs to be emphasized, however, that I am not arguing that mixed strategies are generally optimal in two-person, nonconstant-sum games without detection but, rather, that the introduction of detection probabilities in such games may render mixed strategies appropriate within an expected-payoff game-theoretic framework.

I shall proceed first by defining a generic 2 × 2 game I call the "Truth Game," based on strict ordinal rankings of the outcomes by the two players that satisfy specified primary and secondary goals. Then, assuming particular cardinal utilities/payoffs consistent with these

4. Thomas C. Schelling, *The Strategy of Conflict* (Cambridge, MA: Harvard University Press, 1960).

5. Donald M. Snow, *The Nuclear Future: Toward a Strategy of Uncertainty* (University, AL: University of Alabama Press, 1983).

rankings, I shall illustrate a number of propositions about optimal mixed inducement and guarantee strategies on the part of each player that hold for the Truth Game generally. I shall conclude with some remarks on the relevance of these propositions to current strategic doctrine and the ethical issues raised about acting arbitrarily.

4.2. The Truth Game

In the Truth Game, assume that a *signaler* (S) must choose between telling the truth and lying and, after S has made this choice, a *detector* (D) must then decide to believe him or not. Their choices, then, are not simultaneous. Yet, though S is assumed to choose prior to D, this game cannot be modeled as one of sequential play with perfect information, because I assume that D cannot tell for certain whether S was truthful or not. Thus, D cannot respond to S's strategy by always choosing his better strategy (believe or not believe) associated with S's prior strategy choice (be truthful or lie). Since D is unsure which strategy S chose (later I shall assume that he can make predictions by consulting his detection equipment), the Truth Game is technically a *game of imperfect information,* though both players are assumed to have complete information about the payoffs shown in figure 4.1.

FIGURE 4.1   The Truth Game

		Detector (D)	
		Believe (B)	Do not believe (B̄)
Signaler (S)	Tell truth (T)	(a_2,b_4) ← Truth believed (strong verification) ↓	(a_3,b_2) Truth disbelieved (weak falsification) ↑
	Do not tell truth (T̄)	(a_4,b_1) → Lie believed (strong falsification)	(a_1,b_3) Lie disbelieved (weak verification)

Key: (a_i,b_j) = (payoff to S, payoff to D)
  a_4,b_4 = best payoffs, a_3,b_3 = next-best payoffs; a_2,b_2 = next-worst payoffs; a_1,b_1 = worst payoffs

Assume these payoffs are cardinal utilities, where a_4 and b_4 are the best outcomes for S and D, respectively, a_1 and b_1 the worst. Thus, as before, the higher the subscripts, the better the payoffs for the players, though the subscripts indicate only the rankings of these payoffs by the players and not the utilities, (a_i, b_j), that they associate with each outcome. Optimality calculations, with numerical values for the payoffs, will be illustrated later.

Implicit in the rankings of the outcomes by S and D are the following goals.

S: *Primary Goal*—wants to *hide* the truth or lack thereof (two best outcomes off main diagonal)
   Secondary Goal—prefers to be believed
D: *Primary Goal*—wants to *discover* the truth or lack thereof (two best outcomes on main diagonal)
   Secondary goal—prefers S to be truthful

The primary and secondary goals of each player *completely* specify their ordering of outcomes from best to worst: yes/no answers for each player and each goal automatically rank the four cells of a 2×2 game (a tertiary goal would rank the eight cells of a $2 \times 2 \times 2$ game). This is an example of a lexicographic decision rule, whereby outcomes are ordered first on the basis of a most important criterion (primary goal), then a next most important criterion (secondary goal), and so on.[6]

In S's case, the primary goal establishes that he prefers outcomes off the main diagonal, where he lies and is believed (a_4) or tells the truth and is not believed (a_3). In either case, S succeeds in hiding the truth, whereas on the main diagonal the truth is discovered, either because S tells the truth and is believed (a_2) or lies and is not believed (a_1). The secondary goal establishes that, between the outcomes on and off the main diagonal, S prefers those associated with D's believing (first column) over not believing (second column).

In D's case, the primary goal says that he prefers outcomes on the main diagonal (b_4 and b_3), where he succeeds in discovering the truth, to those off the main diagonal (b_2 and b_1), where he is foiled in his attempt to uncover the truth. The secondary goal says that, between the

6. Peter C. Fishburn, "Lexicographic Orders, Utilities and Decision Rules: A Survey," *Management Science* 20 (July 1974):1442–71.

outcomes on and off the main diagonal, D prefers those associated with S's being truthful (first row) over those associated with S's lying (second row).

In the superpower arms race, these seem reasonable goals to impute to the two sides insofar as each desires to gain an edge over the other or simply wishes to maintain parity if it thinks the other side may be cheating. This may be a cynical view of the motives of each superpower in the nuclear arms race and, from a normative perspective, an undesirable one. Nevertheless, the suspicions of each side probably drive each to try to cover up what exactly it is doing in certain areas, which gives rise to a natural counterdesire on the part of the other side to unmask the possible cover-up.

Each side, of course, knows that certain activities it wants to hide may be detected, so it cannot be certain that its cover-up will succeed. Yet, this fact does not invalidate its having the goals attributed to it, though, as I shall show, its optimal strategy choices will be affected by its realization that, as S, it can be detected with a specified probability by D, and as D, this probability governs its success in realizing its goals in responding to S.[7]

I shall say more later about how well optimal strategies in the Truth Game seem to model the verification problem in the superpower arms race. But I am not so wedded to this particular game as to presume that there are no other candidates that might be descriptive of the clash of goals over verification. For example, the same methodology that I shall describe could be applied to a game in which a_2 and a_3 in the Truth Game are interchanged, making belief in the truth preferable to disbelief for S as well as D and thereby downgrading the importance for S of deceiving D.

It is worth noting that as a hide/discover-the-truth game, with a secondary emphasis on S's desire to be believed and D's desire that S be truthful, the Truth Game enables one not only to distinguish "verification" (main-diagonal outcomes) from "falsification" (off-diagonal outcomes). In addition, it suggests a "strong" and "weak" distinction in each of these main categories (see figure 4.1). Thus, I consider

7. This game is adapted to the problem of monitoring environmental pollution, in a repeated-game extension, in Clifford S. Russell, "Monitoring Sources of Pollution: Lessons from Single and Multiple Play Games," Discussion Paper 121, Quality of the Environment Division (Washington, DC: Resources for the Future, May 1984).

verification stronger when one believes the truth than when one disbelieves a lie, because "the truth" is still unclear in the latter case—one may still not know what to believe, indicating nonfalsification more than verification. Similarly, falsification seems stronger when a lie is believed than when the truth is disbelieved, because disbelief in the truth indicates that one has missed the truth but not necessarily that one has been hoodwinked into believing a falsehood.

Note also that, despite the fact that the primary goals of the two players are diametrically opposed in the Truth Game, the game is not one of total conflict: *both* players do better at (a_2, b_4) than at (a_1, b_3), so what one player "wins" the other does not necessarily "lose." Because the payoffs to the two players, and necessarily their sum, are greater at (a_2, b_4) than at (a_1, b_3)—whatever the cardinal utilities one associates with the ordinal rankings of the four outcomes—the Truth Game is not constant-sum but variable-sum and, therefore, one of partial conflict. In addition, the fact that (a_2, b_4) is better for both players than (a_1, b_3), and there is not another outcome better for at least one player and not worse for the other than (a_2, b_4), means that (a_2, b_4) is Pareto-superior, whereas (a_1, b_3) is Pareto-inferior (see section 1.2).

There is no stability in the Truth Game, as the arrows indicating cyclical preferences over the four outcomes in figure 4.1 make evident. S can do immediately better by departing, in the directions shown by the vertical arrows, from (a_2, b_4) and (a_1, b_3), and D can do immediately better by departing, in the directions shown by the horizontal arrows, from (a_4, b_1) and (a_3, b_2). Because one player always has an incentive to depart from every outcome, no outcome is a Nash equilibrium, from which neither player would have an incentive to depart unilaterally (see section 1.2). Neither does this game have a nonmyopic equilibrium (see sections 2.6 and 2.7). On the other hand, if D could predict S's strategy choice with certainty and if S knew this, the game would have an equilibrium if it were played sequentially: S would choose т (tell the truth) and D would respond with в (believe S); each would do worse by departing from these strategies.

S can induce his next-best outcome (a_3), and D his best outcome (b_4), with moving power or staying power, but neither player has threat power in this game (see section 2.3). The power-induced outcomes, however, do not seem particularly meaningful in games of imperfect information, like the Truth Game, for they are based on the presupposition that each player can respond to the other player's strategy choice

FIGURE 4.2   The Truth Game: An Example

		Detector (D)	
		Believe (B)	Do not believe (B̄)
Signaler (S)	Tell truth (T)	(2,10)	(3,7)
	Do not tell truth (T̄)	(10,0)	(0,8)

Key: (a_i, b_j) = (payoff to S, payoff to D)

according to the theory of moves. Yet, the initial strategy choice of S is, by assumption, not known with certainty by D, making the application of this theory more problematic than it was in chapter 2.

To illustrate the first proposition and demonstrate the possibly paradoxical effects of D's detection capability in the Truth Game, assume that the payoffs to the two players are as shown in figure 4.2. These particular payoffs were chosen to illustrate certain points that follow from the calculations to be described shortly; other assignments of cardinal-utility values, consistent with the ordinal rankings of figure 4.1, could be chosen. Observe that the best and worst payoffs of each player are 10 and 0, respectively, whereas the intermediate payoffs are 2 and 3 for S (he associates relatively low value with telling the truth), 7 and 8 for D (he associates relatively high value with being skeptical by not believing). Assume

p = the conditional probability that D's detection of S's strategy choice is correct (that is, that D detects T when S chooses T and detects T̄ when S chooses T̄.)[8]

8. Raymond Dacey and Donald Wittman, in personal communications (July 1983), have indicated that p must be defined with respect to specific events or actions and not just S's strategy choices of truth telling and lying. In the context of arms control, this can easily be done with a plausible scenario. Let S's first strategy of T be interpreted to mean that S reduces his arms (R) *and* tells the truth about his reduction; and let T̄ be interpreted to mean that S does not reduce his arms (R̄) *and* lies that he has. Then p is the probability that D correctly detects R or R̄, which, by assumption, are actions invariably associated with T and T̄, respectively. Since S will always *claim* that he chose R/T, p defines *the probability that D correctly detects whether this claim is truthful or not.* This probability does not depend on whether S claims to be truthful—he always does—but instead on his actions R and R̄, which I assume are equivalent to T and T̄ in the arms-control scenario.

One could distinguish between D's ability to detect т or т̄, with possibly different probabilities, but in the calculation that follows one need not make this distinction to establish the suboptimal consequences for D (as well as for S) when D follows a *tit-for-tat policy* of B/B̄—that is, believes if he detects т, does not believe if he detects т̄—akin to conditional cooperation in section 3.2.

Assume S and D know p and also that D will respond to *his detection* of S's choice of т or т̄ with tit-for-tat. Then, based on the payoffs in figure 4.2, S's expected payoff, E_S, associated with each of his strategies is

$$E_S(\text{т}) = 2p + 3(1 - p) = 3 - p;$$
$$E_S(\text{т̄}) = 10(1 - p) + 0p = 10 - 10p.$$

Lying is rational if $E_S(\text{т̄}) > E_S(\text{т})$, or

$$10 - 10p > 3 - p$$
$$p < \tfrac{7}{9} = 0.78.$$

For purposes of illustration, assume $p = \tfrac{3}{4} = 0.75$. Then it is rational for S to lie, yielding

$$E_S(\text{т̄}) = (10)(\tfrac{1}{4}) + (0)(\tfrac{3}{4}) = \tfrac{10}{4} = 2.50,$$

which compares with

$$E_S(\text{т}) = (2)(\tfrac{3}{4}) + 3(\tfrac{1}{4}) = \tfrac{9}{4} = 2.25,$$

for being truthful under tit-for-tat.

Now when S lies, D, using his detection equipment, will correctly detect т̄ three-fourths of the time and incorrectly detect т one-fourth of the time; so D's tit-for-tat policy will yield him

$$E_D(\text{tit-for-tat}) = (8)(\tfrac{3}{4}) + (0)(\tfrac{1}{4}) = \tfrac{24}{4} = 6.00.$$

Hence, S does worse than his next-*best* payoff of 3, and D does worse than his next-*worst* payoff of 7. Comparatively speaking, then, D ranks his expected payoff lower than S does, but quantitatively D does much better than S (assuming their utilities are measured on the same scale and can be compared).

Based on the payoffs in the figure 4.2 game, I shall next illustrate the following proposition:

PROPOSITION 4.1. *There may be a mixed strategy that D can adopt, independent of his detection probability* p = $\frac{3}{4}$, *such that if S responds optimally to it, both players will benefit over what they would obtain when D chooses tit-for-tat and S responds optimally to this policy.*

I have already calculated the expected payoffs of D's tit-for-tat policy when $p = \frac{3}{4}$. Now assume D follows a *mixed strategy* $(m, 1 - m)$, where

m = probability that D chooses believe (B),
$1 - m$ = probability that D chooses do not believe (B̄).

Note that m and $1 - m$ are *unconditional probabilities:* they take no account of p; in effect, D ignores his detection equipment.

The difference, Δ, between the expected payoff to S of telling the truth and lying is

$$\Delta = E_S(T) - E_S(\bar{T}).$$

For a given m and the payoffs in figure 4.2,

$$\Delta = [2m + 3(1 - m)] - [10m + 0(1 - m)]$$
$$= [3 - m] - 10m = 3 - 11m.$$

Thus, $\Delta > 0$ iff (if and only if) $m < \frac{3}{11}$. If $m = (\frac{3}{11})^-$, where the minus superscript indicates m is slightly less than $\frac{3}{11}$, it is rational for S to choose T, yielding

$$E_S(T) = 3 - (\tfrac{3}{11})^- = (\tfrac{30}{11})^+ = 2.73^+,$$

where the plus superscript indicates $E_S(T)$ is slightly greater than 2.73. Observe that this value for $E_S(T)$ under mixed strategy $(m, 1 - m)$ exceeds $E_S(\bar{T}) = 10 - 10p$ under tit-for-tat iff $p > \frac{8}{11} = 0.73$.

Given that S chooses T, D's expected payoff from using his mixed strategy is

$$E_D(m) = 10m + 7(1 - m) = 7 + 3m;$$

when $m = (\frac{3}{11})^-$,

$$E_D[(\tfrac{3}{11})^-] = 7 + 3(\tfrac{3}{11})^- = (\tfrac{86}{11})^- = 7.82^-.$$

Clearly, these expected payoffs for S (2.73^+) and D (7.82^-) are better than their expected payoffs under tit-for-tat (2.50 and 6.00, respectively), illustrating Proposition 4.1 (when $0.73 < p < 0.78$). Also note that the (3,7) outcome in the figure 4.2 game is Pareto-superior to the tit-for-tat expected payoffs, but this outcome is not in equilibrium, as noted earlier.

The mixed-strategy expected payoffs for S and D are based on the assumption that D chooses $m < \frac{3}{11}$ to induce S to tell the truth. What are the consequences for D if he chooses $m > \frac{3}{11}$ to induce S to lie? In this case, given that S rationally chooses Ŧ, D's expected payoff is

$$E_D(m) = 0(m) + 8(1 - m) = 8 - 8m;$$

when $m = (\frac{3}{11})^+$,

$$E_D[(\tfrac{3}{11})^+] = 8 - 8(\tfrac{3}{11})^+ = (\tfrac{64}{11})^- = 5.82^-,$$

which is substantially less than the expected payoff D obtains (7.82^-) when he makes it advantageous for S to be truthful. Moreover, 5.82^- is less than the 6.00 that D obtains from tit-for-tat, so Proposition 4.1 does not hold if D randomizes his choices between B and B̄ to induce S to lie.

In sum, I have shown that both players lose when D sticks punctiliously to a policy of tit-for-tat that makes it advantageous for S to lie. Both can do better, by comparison, when D ignores his detection equipment entirely and randomizes his choices between B and B̄ to induce S to be truthful.

This mixed-strategy calculation raises the question of how D might persuade S that it is indeed in both players' interest that D randomize his choices—in the prescribed manner—to elicit truth telling from S. Before addressing this question, however, I shall demonstrate that it is not in general optimal for D totally to ignore the signal his detection equipment gives him. Instead, he should incorporate this information into his inducement calculations, which will be described next using a more sophisticated model.

4.3. Optimal Inducement Strategies

I begin by complicating the previous model. Let

q = probability that D chooses B if his detector indicates T;

r = probability that D chooses B if his detector indicates Ŧ.

Previously I assumed that $q = 1$ and $r = 0$ when D followed tit-for-tat, but now I want to show that it is optimal in the figure 4.2 Truth Game for D to respond to his detector (still assumed to have reliability $p = \frac{3}{4}$, whatever S chooses) probabilistically rather than deterministically.

Let

$$s = \text{probability that S chooses T.}$$

Then for $0 \leq q,r,s \leq 1$, S's and D's expected payoffs are

$$E_S = sE_S(\text{T}) + (1 - s)E_S(\bar{\text{T}})$$
$$= s\{p[qa_2 + (1 - q)a_3] + (1 - p)[ra_2 + (1 - r)a_3]\}$$
$$+ (1 - s)\{p[ra_4 + (1 - r)a_1] + (1 - p)[qa_4$$
$$+ (1 - q)a_1]\};$$

$$E_D = sE_D(\text{T}) + (1 - s)E_D(\bar{\text{T}})$$
$$= s\{p[qb_4 + (1 - q)b_2] + (1 - p)[rb_4 + (1 - r)b_2]\}$$
$$+ (1 - s)\{p[rb_1 + (1 - r)b_3] + (1 - p)[qb_1$$
$$+ (1 - q)b_3]\}.$$

For the payoffs given in the figure 4.2 game, the expected payoffs (after considerable simplification) are

$$E_S = (\tfrac{1}{4})[s(12 - 13q - 31r) + 30r + 10q]; \tag{4.1}$$

$$E_D = (\tfrac{1}{4})[s(-4 + 17q + 27r) - 24r - 8q + 32]. \tag{4.2}$$

Now, by keeping $(12 - 13q - 31r)$ positive, D can induce S to tell the truth, because doing so will raise E_S, given $s > 0$.

In particular, if $r = 0$ and $q = (\tfrac{12}{13})^-$, S should always tell the truth ($s = 1$), yielding

$$E_S = (\tfrac{30}{13})^+ = 2.31^+.$$

Similarly, D's expected payoff will be

$$E_D = (\tfrac{118}{13})^- = 9.08^-.$$

The fact that 9.08^- is greater than what D would obtain from his "straight" mixed strategy (7.82^-)—independent of what he detects—or tit-for-tat (6.00)—described in section 4.2—seems a good reason for adopting the inducement strategy described in the previous paragraph. That S's expected payoff of 2.31^+ is less than what he obtains from D's mixed strategy (2.73^+) or tit-for-tat (2.50) means that S suffers when he (rationally) responds to the incentive D offers him to be truthful.

D's inducement strategy in this case is a more sophisticated policy than simply tit-for-tat. That is, when D makes his strategy choices probabilistic—according to q and r given above—he can do considerably better and, at the same time, decrease S's expected payoff. (That these values are indeed optimal is shown in the Appendix to this chapter.)

The key to this optimality calculation is that D can induce S to choose т over т̄—but not just by choosing a (straight) mixed strategy, unrelated to what he detects. Rather, D should only selectively follow the signals of his detector, according to the calculated q and r optimality values given earlier, though it has a relatively high reliability $p = \frac{3}{4}$. Thus, if D's detection equipment indicates that S chose т̄, it is optimal for D always to choose b̄ (as expected), but if it indicates that S chose т, it is optimal for D to choose b only about $\frac{12}{13} = 92$ percent of the time.

Of course, when $p = 1$ and D's detection capability is perfect, he should strictly adhere to tit-for-tat. But then S should always tell the truth, because his payoff for truth-telling will be 2 versus 0 for lying; this, in turn, gives D his highest payoff of 10, so—as indicated earlier—the strategies т and b/b̄ are in equilibrium when detection is certain. In reality, however, this is never the case.

The previous example illustrates the following proposition:

PROPOSITION 4.2. *When D follows a sophisticated inducement strategy (mixed), based on his detection probability, he can raise his expected payoff, and lower S's, over what the players would obtain from tit-for-tat or a straight mixed strategy.*

Note that this sophisticated inducement strategy, dependent on whether D detects т or т̄, is itself mixed. If D detects т̄, he should always choose b̄ (as with tit-for-tat); the mixing comes in only when D detects т—and 8 percent of the time does not respond with b.

This deviation by D from tit-for-tat simultaneously lowers $E_S(\bar{\text{т}})$, and raises $E_S(\text{т})$, for S in order to induce him to choose т. But this means that S receives less than tit-for-tat would give him at the same time that D gains more. This reasoning applies generally in the Truth

Game, whatever the numerical payoffs are that are consistent with the rankings in figure 4.1, so Proposition 4.2 is not specific to the figure 4.2 payoffs but characterizes all Truth Games in which lying is rational when D follows tit-for-tat (see Appendix). A sophisticated inducement strategy, by incorporating D's detection probability in the expected-payoff calculations, entices S to be truthful—to his detriment and D's benefit.

One might think in the earlier optimality calculation for E_S that one could keep the factor $(12 - 13q - 31r)$ in equation (4.1) positive by letting $q = 1$ instead of $r = 0$. But if $q = 1$, the factor becomes $(-1 - 31r)$, which can be made positive only if $r < 0$; this strategic choice by D, however, is ruled out by the fact that r is a probability and, therefore, cannot be negative. (As shown in the Appendix, to maximize E_D, D should choose q and r, which are in an inverse linear relationship to each other, so that the former is as large and the latter as small as possible, given that certain conditions are met.) In the figure 4.2 example, setting $r = 0$ means that only q is allowed to vary, so optimal mixing can occur only when D detects т and not when he detects т̄.

But if D can take advantage of his detection capability to induce S to be truthful in order to help himself (D), why cannot S, whom I assume also knows this capability, choose a mixed strategy to induce D to believe him—and in the process raise his own expected payoff? The answer is that he can; I shall illustrate how, after stating a third proposition (analogous to Proposition 4.2):

PROPOSITION 4.3. *When S follows a sophisticated inducement strategy (mixed), based on D's detection probability, he can raise his expected payoff, and lower D's, over what the players would obtain from tit-for-tat or a straight mixed strategy.*

Consider equation (4.2) for E_D. It can be rewritten as

$$E_D = (\tfrac{1}{4})[q(17s - 8) + r(27s - 24) + (-4s + 32)].   (4.3)$$

Clearly, when $s = (\tfrac{8}{17})^+$, D will have an incentive to set $q = 1$ (and $r = 0$) to maximize E_D; but when $s = (\tfrac{24}{27})^+ = (\tfrac{8}{9})^+$, he will now have an incentive to set $r = 1$ as well. In the former case, $E_S = (\tfrac{81}{34})^+ = 2.38^+$, and in the latter case $E_S = (\tfrac{26}{9})^+ = 2.89^+$, so S would prefer the latter. This gives D an expected payoff of $E_D = (\tfrac{65}{9})^- = 7.22^-$, compared with $(\tfrac{128}{17})^- = 7.53^-$ in the former case.

Thus, to induce D always to choose в—whether S chooses т ($q = 1$)

or $\bar{\text{T}}$ ($r = 1$)—S should adopt a mixed strategy (t, $1 - t$) over T and $\bar{\text{T}}$, where $t > \frac{8}{9} = 0.89$. In other words, if S is truthful about 90 percent of the time, it is in D's interest always to believe S, whatever signal he detects.

This is the sophisticated inducement strategy (mixed), alluded to in Proposition 4.3, that is optimal in the figure 4.2 example. I showed above that, if $t > \frac{8}{9}$, this strategy is better for S than tit-for-tat (which is optimal when $\frac{8}{17} < p \leq \frac{8}{9}$), so it remains only to show that it is better for S than a straight mixed strategy.

A straight mixed strategy is one in which S would choose probability t of telling the truth such that $E_D(\text{B}) > E_D(\bar{\text{B}})$ for D, or

$$10t + 0(1 - t) > 7t + 8(1 - t)$$

$$t > \tfrac{8}{11}.$$

If, for example, $t = (\frac{8}{11})^+ = 0.73^+$ and D rationally responds by always choosing B, the expected payoff to S will be

$$E_S = 2t + 10(1 - t) = 10 - 8t,$$

or $10 - 8(\frac{8}{11})^+ = (\frac{24}{11})^+ = 2.18^-$, which is well below the 2.89^+ expected payoff S obtains when D's detection capability is incorporated into his calculation of an optimal inducement strategy.

In summary, I have shown that when D induces S always to be truthful,

$$E_S = 2.31^+ \text{ and } E_D = 9.08^-;$$

when S induces D always to believe,

$$E_S = 2.89^+ \text{ and } E_D = 7.22^-.$$

There is obviously a value to "leading" the other player with a sophisticated inducement strategy, which in general will be mixed.

If both players choose their inducement strategies simultaneously, both suffer compared with what each's inducement strategy would yield when the other player optimally responds to it (D suffers less because S, by being truthful 89 percent of the time, comes close to doing what D would like him to do):

$$E_S = 2.31, E_D = 8.96.$$

These results suggest that should one player not be able successfully to assert his leadership, it may not be in that player's best interest to pursue an inducement strategy. Instead, he may prefer to guarantee himself an expected payoff independent of what the other player does. This is the topic explored in section 4.4.

4.4. Optimal Guarantee Strategies and Overall Comparisons

Strategies that guarantee each player an expected payoff not dependent on the other player's strategy choice in the Truth Game (with detection) are analogous to minimax/maximin strategies that guarantee the value in two-person, constant-sum games (without detection). The difference lies in the fact that *either* player's guarantee strategy in a constant-sum game guarantees the other player's (guarantee) payoff, for the guarantee—and all other—payoffs to the players must sum to the constant. In the Truth Game, by contrast, the guarantee strategy of one player does not determine the other player's payoff, which depends on the latter's choice. This leads to the fourth (and last) proposition:

PROPOSITION 4.4. *S and D can guarantee themselves expected payoffs, independent of the strategy choice of the other player, which are in general lower than the expected payoffs they obtain from their sophisticated inducement strategies.*

D can make his expected payoff independent of s in equation (4.2) by letting

$$-4 + 17q + 27r = 0.$$

In particular, if $r = 0$, $q = \frac{4}{17}$, giving $E_D = \frac{128}{17} = 7.53$, a security value of which D can be assured whatever strategy S chooses. In this case, S does best to pick strategy T and obtain an expected payoff of $\frac{48}{17} = 2.82$. Note that D's security value of 7.53 is substantially below his inducement value of 9.08^-.

Now consider the game from S's perspective. To see how S can make his expected payoff independent of the choice of q and r by D, rewrite equation (4.1) as follows:

$$E_S = (\tfrac{1}{4}) [q(-13s + 10) + r(-31s + 30) + 12s]. \quad (4.4)$$

This equation is analogous to equation (4.3)—which itself is a rewrite of equation (4.2)—in section 4.3.

Now S can make E_S independent of q by choosing $s = \frac{10}{13}$, or independent of r by choosing $s = \frac{30}{31}$. In the former case, his expected payoff will be

$$E_S = (\tfrac{1}{4})[r(-\tfrac{310}{13} + 30) + \tfrac{120}{13}]$$
$$= r(\tfrac{20}{13}) + \tfrac{30}{13}.$$

Clearly, if $r = 0$—its minimum value—S can guarantee himself $\frac{30}{13} = 2.31$. By comparison, in the latter case,

$$E_S = (\tfrac{1}{4})[q(-\tfrac{390}{31} + 10) + \tfrac{360}{31}]$$
$$= q(-\tfrac{20}{31}) + \tfrac{90}{31}.$$

If $q = 1$—its maximum value—S can guarantee himself $\frac{70}{31} = 2.26$. Hence, S can do better by making E_S independent of q by choosing $s = \frac{10}{13}$. Then, as I showed in section 4.3, D will have an incentive to set $q = 1$ and $r = 0$, yielding an expected payoff for D of $\frac{17}{2} = 8.50$. As with D's security value, S's security value of 2.31 is well below his inducement value of 2.89^+.

Since security values are independent of the other player's strategy choice (that is, of a choice of s by S and choices of q and r by D), they are the same for S (2.31) and D (8.50), whatever their opponents do. As with optimal mixed strategies in two-person, constant-sum games, a player's choice of a guarantee strategy means that he may not benefit from possible "mistakes" by his opponent. (This is always true of D but not of S, who benefits if $r > 0$ when $s = \frac{10}{13}$.)

A more general picture emerges when one compares the expected payoffs of the two players in the Truth Game for their different strategy pairs shown in table 4.1. To begin with, D's adherence to tit-for-tat hurts both players in this game, as was shown in section 4.2, despite D's relatively high detection probability of $p = \frac{3}{4}$ and S's knowledge of it. The tit-for-tat policy is less desirable because this p is not high enough to encourage truth-telling by S, whereas a straight mixed strategy by D—ignoring what he detects—that makes it rational for S to be truthful in fact benefits both players. Thus, tit-for-tat by D, coupled with lying by S, is Pareto-inferior to the second set of strategies shown in table 4.1

TABLE 4.1 Expected Payoffs of Different Strategy Pairs in the Truth Game ($p = \frac{3}{4}$)

Strategy Pair	Signaler (S)	Detector (D)	Pareto-inferior*
Tit-for-tat by D, lying by S	2.50	6.00	Yes
Straight mixed by D, truth-telling by S	2.73+	7.82−	No
Sophisticated inducement by D, truth telling by S	2.31+	9.08−	No
Sophisticated inducement by S, always believing by D	2.89+	7.22−	No
Sophisticated inducement by S and D	2.31	8.96	Yes
Guarantee by D, truth telling by S	2.82	7.53	No
Guarantee by S, tit-for-tat by D	2.31	8.50	Yes
Guarantee by S and D	2.31	7.53	Yes

*Pareto-inferiority is based only on the numerical payoffs, not the pluses or minuses.

(straight mixed strategy by D, truth-telling by S), so rational players would presumably not subscribe to the first strategies.

At the same time, it would seem foolish for D to throw away the information he obtains from his detection equipment and choose a straight mixed strategy to induce S to be truthful. In fact, D can use his detection capability to concoct a sophisticated inducement strategy that, while it makes it rational for S still to tell the truth, benefits him (D) even more, though now at S's expense.

But there is no rule in the Truth Game that says that only D can be the initiator. If S can turn the tables, inducing D always to believe by being truthful approximately 90 percent of the time, S now benefits at D's expense.

Both players achieve their highest expected payoffs (2.89+ for S, 9.08− for D) by exploiting the known reliability of the detection equipment and using mixed strategies to induce the other player to make a particular choice favorable to themselves. It is not surprising that D wants S to be truthful, nor is it surprising that S wants D to ignore his detection equipment completely and always believe him (S), regardless of the signal he (D) detects.

What is unexpected is that S, by being truthful almost all the time, can make it rational for D always to believe him, even when he (D) detects lying. Manifestly, there is a value in S's establishing a record of honesty, because then his reputation may sustain D's belief even when D's detector indicates lying. Thereby *implicit* belief, or trust, in S— believing S regardless of what he detects—may be a rational response for D.

The major problem I see with inducement strategies—even sophisticated ones that incorporate detection information to induce rational responses—is that the putative responder may not want to be induced. Indeed, as the expected payoffs demonstrate, it is always better for him to seize the initiative himself than passively respond to the incentives the other player sets up for him with his mixed strategy.

Unless one player can lay valid claim to being the initiator rather than the responder, I suspect that there will be a conflict over proper roles—as well there should be, since it is rational for the players to fight for the initiative. The issue of who defers to whom can partially be circumvented by the guarantee strategies, but they limit the players to relatively low fixed expected payoffs (2.31 for S, 7.53 for D). Curiously, the other player's optimal response to these strategies—tit-for-tat by D, truth-telling by S—provides each of them with higher expected payoffs (2.82 for S, 8.50 for D) than were they the guarantors. When both players try simultaneously to induce or guarantee, the resulting outcomes are Pareto-inferior, though inducement is better for D than guarantee in this case.

In summary, it pays to be responsive to a guarantor but not an inducer, who will capitalize on your responsiveness. In the latter case, you can do at least as well and generally better as a guarantor yourself (7.53 versus 7.22$^-$ for D, 2.31 in either case for S).

The fact, however, that S's sophisticated inducement strategy yields him at least as much as his guarantee strategy, and sometimes more (if D is responsive), means that it dominates his guarantee strategy and should always be chosen over it. D, in turn, does best by responding with his own inducement strategy, yielding 2.31 and 8.96 for S and D, respectively. On the other hand, if S should be responsive to D's sophisticated inducement strategy, D does even better (9.08), making his inducement strategy dominant as well.

Note that four strategy pairs in table 4.1 are Pareto-superior and four are Pareto-inferior. The former are the best candidates for *both* players, though D's straight mixed strategy (second row in table 4.1) ignores information it seems unlikely the players would eschew. For reasons given in the previous paragraph, however, the fifth-row pair seems particularly attractive since each player has an incentive to induce the other, regardless of how the other responds. Unfortunately for D, however, this is a Pareto-inferior pair because he suffers somewhat (8.96 versus 9.08) when S, who has no incentive to switch from sophisticated inducement, is not truth-telling.

In section 4.5, I turn to the question of interpreting these theoretical results. I shall argue that the verification problem in arms control, particularly between the superpowers, very much involves inducements and guarantees that, as in the Truth Game, may require paying only selective attention to one's detection equipment by D, occasional lying by S.

4.5. Interpretation and Conclusions

I have established four propositions that give better and worse strategies for a signaler and a detector—as measured by their expected payoffs—in the Truth Game. The last three propositions hold generally, whatever the cardinal utilities associated with the preference rankings in the Truth Game are, as long as D's detection probability is low enough to make lying rational for S when D follows a tit-for-tat policy. The first proposition also requires that this detection probability be within a certain range (see Appendix).

Patently, policymakers in some areas of national defense have considered lying and other forms of less-than-forthcoming behavior rational, presumably because they thought the chances of detection were sufficiently low that the risk of being discovered made such behavior worthwhile. I believe the Truth Game, insofar as it mirrors the goals of a policymaker choosing between telling and not telling the truth, illustrates why this may be the case.

The Truth Game also illustrates how a detector might try to coax out the truth. In general, he (D) should *not* always believe his detection equipment, and respond accordingly (that is, with tit-for-tat), even if it is fairly reliable. It is better instead to pay only selective attention to it, sometimes believing it when it indicates a lie, sometimes not believing an indication of the truth. Only the latter denial, however, is rational in the illustrative game, but it makes the point that this apparently errant behavior may be what is required to make truth-telling rational for S.

Optimal guarantee strategies that elicit the truth are also mixed, as are inducement and guarantee strategies that S may invoke. Perhaps the strangest result is that largely honest behavior on S's part may make it rational for D not to trust his detection equipment, even when it indicates lying, but instead always to believe S (at least until S's impeccable reputation for truthfulness is undermined).

In the superpower arms race, it seems, both sides have, by and large, been willing to give each other the benefit of the doubt—at least until recently[9]—despite contrary indications they sometimes receive (and which are considered by the US-USSR Standing Consultative Commission).[10] This is an example of paying only selective attention to one's detection equipment, especially when the other side is viewed as a mostly honest signaler.

It also seems that both sides occasionally disbelieve what are perceived to be truthful signals, perhaps to generate better evidence from the other side. As optimal inducement and guarantee strategies of D in the Truth Game suggest, this behavior is eminently rational when it makes S more forthcoming.

It appears, then, that the superpowers probably do not always play it "straight" about what they detect.[11] Whether they deliberately mix things up, or act as if they do, their sometimes capricious behavior seems consistent with optimal mixed strategies in the Truth Game.

Of course, fine-grained optimality calculations, based on the cardinal utilities of the players and their detection probabilities, cannot be made with any exactitude in most real-world applications. Yet, these calculations do show up important qualitative differences between, say,

9. Tom Wicker, "Cheating on SALT," *New York Times,* May 3, 1983, p. A27; and Bernard Gwertzman, "Reagan Is Said to Find Breaches by Soviets of Agreements on Arms," *New York Times,* January 14, 1984, p. 1.

10. Robert W. Buchheim and Dan Caldwell, "The US-USSR Standing Consultative Commission: Description and Appraisal" (Center for Foreign Policy Development, Brown University, 1983, mimeographed).

11. Jeffrey T. Richelson, "The Keyhole Satellite Program," *Journal of Strategic Studies* 7, no. 2 (June 1984):212–53; and Gerald M. Steinberg, *Satellite Reconnaissance: The Role of Informal Bargaining* (New York: Praeger, 1983).

inducement and guarantee strategies. The fact that both kinds of optimal strategies are mixed in a nonconstant-sum game like the Truth Game seems to me most significant.

At a normative level, the optimality of mixed strategies indicates that one should always act probabilistically—randomizing one's choices within certain constraints—though this behavior is, in a fundamental sense, arbitrary. Anomalously, arbitrariness may be required to satisfy exemplary goals, such as discovering the truth. Hence, one should not shun it if optimal achievement of these goals is desired. At the same time, arbitrary behavior may clash with well-known ethical principles and, in a theological context, raises the distressing problem of evil in the world.[12]

In the secular arena of arms control, nonadherence to tit-for-tat—under prescribed conditions—may be viewed as a kind of deliberate deception or clandestine behavior, which has been previously analyzed in 2 × 2 ordinal games using a different model[13] and is illustrated in section 2.3. The moral issue, I believe, is whether the end of seeking the truth, or protecting oneself in an arms race, provides sufficient justification for S's occasional lying or for D's faking his response (by departing from tit-for-tat) to the signal of S he detects.[14]

The issue seems to me not clear-cut, especially given the fact that detection is never perfect. This compromises any attempt to benefit from always being truthful (S) or adhering meticulously to a reciprocity principle like tit-for-tat (D). More generally, simple ethical positions in an uncertain world become more tenuous.

12. Steven J. Brams, *Superior Beings: If They Exist, How Would We Know? Game-Theoretic Implications of Omniscience, Omnipotence, Immortality, and Incomprehensibility* (New York: Springer-Verlag, 1983).

13. Steven J. Brams, "Deception in 2 × 2 Games," *Journal of Peace Science* 2 (Spring 1977):171–203. Other game-theoretic and related models, relevant to problems of detection addressed in this and the previous chapter, are developed in Robert Axelrod, "The Rational Timing of Surprise," *World Politics* 31, no. 2 (January 1979):228–46; R. Axelrod, "Coping with Deception," in *Applied Game Theory: Proceedings of a Conference of the Institute for Advanced Studies, Vienna, June 13–16, 1978*, ed. S. J. Brams, A. Schotter, and G. Schwödiauer (Würzburg, West Germany: Physica-Verlag, 1979), pp. 390–405; and William Reese, "Deception in a Game Theoretic Framework," in *Strategic Military Deception*, ed. Donald C. Daniel and Katherine L. Herbig (New York: Pergamon, 1982), pp. 115–35.

14. Sissela Bok, *Lying: Moral Choice in Public and Private Life* (New York: Pantheon, 1978).

Appendix

I shall first sketch a proof of why, whenever lying is rational for S in the Truth Game under tit-for-tat, D can always do better with a sophisticated inducement strategy than with tit-for-tat, whatever the cardinal utilities associated with the ordinal ranks in the figure 4.1 game are. Recall that, for the utilities assumed in the figure 4.2 payoff matrix, in moving from tit-for-tat to sophisticated inducement D lowered q from 1 to $\frac{12}{13}$ but let r remain 0.

In general, lowering q in the figure 4.1 game but keeping $r = 0$ (its minimum value), will have two effects on S's expected payoff:

1. If S chose T, it gives more weight to a_3 than a_2 if D correctly detects T; if D incorrectly detects T̄, the effect is the same as tit-for-tat;
2. If S chose T̄, it gives more weight to a_1 than a_4 if D incorrectly detects T; if D correctly detects T̄, the effect is the same as tit-for-tat.

Effect (1) increases S's expected payoff from choosing T, whereas effect (2) decreases his expected payoff from choosing T̄. Necessarily, in continuously lowering q, there is some threshold value $q < 1$ at which $E_S(T) = E_S(\bar{T})$, occurring when:

$$p[qa_2 + (1 - q)a_3] + (1 - p)a_3 = pa_1 + (1 - p)[qa_4 + (1 - q)a_1],$$

or

$$q = \frac{(a_1 - a_3)}{(a_1 - a_4) + p(-a_1 + a_2 - a_3 + a_4)}. \tag{A1}$$

Call this threshold value q'. At q', S's expected payoffs from telling the truth and lying are the same, but D's expected payoffs from inducing S to be truthful and to lie are

$$E_D(T) = p[q'b_4 + (1 - q')b_2] + (1 - p)b_2; \tag{A2}$$

$$E_D(\bar{T}) = pb_3 + (1 - p)[q'b_1 + (1 - q')b_3]. \tag{A3}$$

By contrast,

$$E_D(\text{tit-for-tat}) = pb_3 + (1 - p)b_1. \tag{A4}$$

The right-hand side of equation (A3) is clearly greater than the right-hand side of equation (A4), so

$$E_D(\bar{\text{T}}) > E_D(\text{tit-for-tat}).$$

Now D can choose between $E_D(\text{T})$ and $E_D(\bar{\text{T}})$; assume he will choose whichever is greater. In fact, by slightly lowering q', he can induce S to choose T, obtaining essentially $E_D(\text{T})$; or by slightly raising q', he can induce S to choose $\bar{\text{T}}$, obtaining essentially $E_D(\bar{\text{T}})$. [Larger decreases and increases will diminish $E_D(\text{T})$ and $E_D(\bar{\text{T}})$, respectively, from their maximal values at $q = q'$.]

Without knowing q' and D's payoff values, one cannot say whether D will prefer to induce T or $\bar{\text{T}}$ [compare the right-hand sides of equations (A2) and (A3)]. But since $E_D(\bar{\text{T}})$ always exceeds $E_D(\text{tit-for-tat})$, by assumption $E_D(\text{T})$ does, too, if D chooses to induce T because $E_D(\text{T}) > E_D(\bar{\text{T}})$. So whichever strategy it is rational for D to induce (T or $\bar{\text{T}}$), sophisticated inducement is always better for D than tit-for-tat, whatever the cardinal utilities associated with the figure 4.1 ordinal ranks are.

So far I have assumed that D would only lower q to make $E_S(\text{T}) = E_S(\bar{\text{T}})$ and then, by perturbing the resulting q' slightly up or down, induce S to choose T or $\bar{\text{T}}$. Could D also produce this effect by raising r from its tit-for-tat value of 0? The answer is yes, because in raising r he would be giving more weight to a_3 than a_2 in the first row of the figure 4.1 payoff matrix (when he incorrectly detects T) and more weight to a_1 than a_4 in the second row (when he correctly detects $\bar{\text{T}}$). Doing either increases $E_S(\text{T})$ over $E_S(\bar{\text{T}})$, which is exactly what is required to equalize these expected payoffs. The question now is: Does D benefit more in lowering q from 1 or raising r from 0?

To answer this question, consider the expected payoffs when S chooses T and $\bar{\text{T}}$:

$$E_D(\text{T}) = p[qb_4 + (1 - q)b_2] + (1 - p)[rb_4 + (1 - r)b_2]$$
$$= (b_4 - b_2)[qp + r(1 - p)] + b_2;$$
$$E_D(\bar{\text{T}}) = p[rb_1 + (1 - r)b_3] + (1 - p)[qb_1 + (1 - p)b_3]$$
$$= (b_1 - b_3)[q(1 - p) + rp] + b_3.$$

Without knowing the numerical values of the payoffs and probabilities, one cannot say whether $E_D(\text{T})$ exceeds $E_D(\bar{\text{T}})$, or vice versa. However, since I assume $p > \frac{1}{2}$ (that is, D's predictive powers are greater than fifty-fifty, or random), the "q" factor in the second expression of $E_D(\text{T})$, p, is greater than the "r" factor, $1 - p$, whereas the reverse is the case for $E_D(\bar{\text{T}})$. If there was a one-to-one trade-off between q and r, then D, to maximize E_D when $E_S(\text{T}) = E_S(\bar{\text{T}})$, would make q as large as possible in the expression for $E_D(\text{T})$ and r as small as possible in the expression for $E_D(\bar{\text{T}})$, since it is multiplied by a negative factor, $b_1 - b_3$ [whereas q in the expression for $E_D(\bar{\text{T}})$ is multiplied by a positive factor, $b_4 - b_2$].

But to make r as small as possible is equivalent to making q as large as possible, for they are in an inverse linear relationship to each other. To wit, all equalizing strategies for which S is indifferent between T and $\bar{\text{T}}$ are given by $E_S(\text{T}) = E_S(\bar{\text{T}})$, or

$$q(-a_4 + a_1 + pA) + r(-a_3 + a_2 - pA) + a_3 - a_1 = 0,$$

where $A = a_4 - a_3 + a_2 - a_1$. $E_S(\text{T}) = E_S(\bar{\text{T}})$ is a straight line with negative slope and q-intercept q', as shown in figure A4.1.(The numerical values for q', the r-intercept, and the slope of the equalizing line are given for the figure 4.2 example in the text.) Also shown in figure A4.1 as the diagonal of the (closed) unit square are the $m = q = r$ "blind" (straight mixed) strategies, which are independent of S's choice of T or $\bar{\text{T}}$.

Clearly, there is an infinite number of values (q,r), $0 \leq q$, $r \leq 1$, along the equalizing line that D might perturb to induce either T or $\bar{\text{T}}$. However, D maximizes E_D by making q as large as possible (that is, $q = q'$) and r as small as possible (that is, $r = 0$)—whether S chooses T or $\bar{\text{T}}$—if $p > r/(q + r)$ and $p > q/(q + r)$. This is because these conditions ensure that $qp > r(1 - p)$ inside the brackets of the second expression of $E_D(\text{T})$ and $(1 - p) > rp$ inside the brackets of the second expression of $E_D(\bar{\text{T}})$. If these inequalities are reversed, then it is rational for D to make q as small as possible and r as large as possible.

In the figure 4.2 numerical example, the negative slope of -0.42 says that for every unit decrease in q, there is a 42 percent unit increase in r. Thus, the above inequalities for this example imply that $p > 0.42/(1 + 0.42) = 0.30$ and $p > 1/(1 + 0.42) = 0.70$, which are met by $p = 0.75$.

FIGURE A4.1   Equalizing and "Blind" (Straight Mixed) Strategies of D in the Truth Game

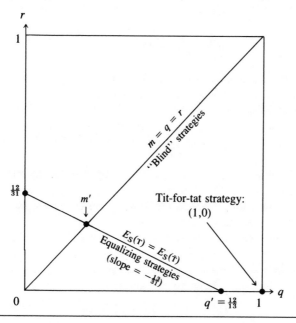

Key: m = probability that D chooses B
q = probability that D chooses B if detector indicates T
r = probability that D chooses B if detector indicates T
m' = value of m such that $E_S(\tau) = E_S(\bar{\tau})$ when $q = r$
q' = value of q such that $E_S(\tau) = E_S(\bar{\tau})$ when $r = 0$
Shaded area indicates those values of (q,r) such that D would want to induce T
Clear area indicates those values of (q,r) such that D would want to induce T
Numerical values of r-intercept, q', and slope are based on payoffs shown in figure 4.2

Next I shall show that D's optimal inducement strategy, which entails lowering q but leaving $r = 0$ (as under tit-for-tat) unchanged, is, for sufficiently high p, better for D than a straight mixed strategy (that is, one independent of the signal he detects). First, to equalize S's expected payoff from telling the truth and lying, D would choose B with probability m and $\bar{\text{B}}$ with probability $(1 - m)$ such that $E_S(\text{T}) = E_S(\bar{\text{T}})$:

$$a_2 m + a_3(1 - m) = a_4 m + a_1(1 - m),$$

or

$$m = \frac{(a_1 - a_3)}{(a_1 - a_4) + (a_2 - a_3)}. \tag{A5}$$

Call this value m', which is the point of intersection of the "blind" (straight mixed) and the equalizing strategy lines in figure A4.1. Now compare the right-hand sides of equations (A1) and (A5). The fractions are the same except for the second terms in the denominator. By assumption, $(a_2 - a_3)$ is always negative in equation (A5), whereas $p[(a_2 - a_1) + (a_4 - a_3)]$ is always positive when p $\neq$ 0 in equation (A1). Because the latter term increases the value of the fraction in equation (A1)—a positive number is added to a larger negative number in the denominator—whereas the former term decreases the value of the fraction in equation (A5), $q' > m'$.

Now one can compare the expected payoffs D can induce with a sophisticated inducement strategy, on the one hand, and a straight mixed strategy on the other. At m', D's expected payoffs from inducing S to be truthful or to lie with a straight mixed strategy are:

$$E_D(\text{T}) = b_4 m' + b_2(1 - m'); \tag{A6}$$

$$E_D(\bar{\text{T}}) = b_1 m' + b_3(1 - m'). \tag{A7}$$

Compare these values of E_D with those given by equations (A2) and (A3), first in the extreme case when $p = 1$. Clearly, since $q' > m'$, D's expected payoff given by equation (A2) is greater than that given by equation (A6). Similarly, comparing equations (A3) and (A7), D's expected payoff given by equation (A3) is greater than that given by equation (A7) when $p = 1$.

As p is lowered from its maximal value of 1, it is easy to show that there is a crossover value (at $p = \frac{8}{11}$ for the figure 4.2 payoffs) when $E_D(\text{T})$ given by equation (A2) equals $E_D(\text{T})$ given by equation (A6). [Crossover also occurs for the $E_D(\bar{\text{T}})$ of equations (A3) and (A7).] Above this value p is sufficiently high for sophisticated inducement to yield a higher expected payoff for D than that yielded by "blind" inducement (that is, the straight mixed strategy).

I have now shown that, for a sufficiently high p, D can do better with sophisticated inducement than by following tit-for-tat or a straight mixed strategy in the ordinal Truth Game of figure 4.2, which proves Proposition 4.2. Proposition 4.1 is dependent not only on p being above a certain minimum ($p > \frac{8}{11}$ for the payoffs in the figure 4.2 game) to ensure that D prefers his straight mixed strategy over tit-for-tat but also on it being below a certain maximum ($p < \frac{7}{9}$ in the figure 4.2 game) to ensure that lying is rational for S when D follows tit-for-tat. Although there is no assurance that, for any cardinal utilities one associates with the ordinal ranks in the figure 4.1 game, the minimum will fall below the maximum, the figure 4.2 example does establish that there are utilities such that a straight mixed strategy can benefit both players over tit-for-tat.

Proposition 4.3 follows from an argument, analogous to that made for Proposition 4.2, that S, like D, can benefit from sophisticated inducement. Proposition 4.4 requires a different argument, which I will not spell out here. In essence, because a guarantee strategy depends only on one's own payoffs, it does not take account of the fact that, in a nonconstant-sum game, it is sometimes in the interest of the other player to help you. Typically, one "throws away value" in choosing only to guarantee a minimum expected payoff. Clearly, a player can benefit over a guarantee strategy by inducing the other player to choose a strategy beneficial to himself (first player), which is a general proposition that applies to nonconstant-sum games other than the Truth Game.

Neither inducement strategies nor guarantee strategies are stable in the sense of Nash:[15] at least one player always has an incentive to depart unilaterally from the outcome defined by these strategies. In the case of inducement, the inducer always has an incentive to depart from his mixed strategy and choose his pure strategy that is optimal against the pure strategy he induces the other player to select. Guarantee strategies are also vulnerable, given an optimal pure-strategy response by the other player. In general, the guarantor will have an optimal pure-strategy counterresponse, and so on, in a cyclical game like the Truth Game.

Nash proved that every finite, two-person game that, like the Truth Game without detection, does not have an equilibrium in pure strategies

15. John Nash, "Non-cooperative Games," *Annals of Mathematics* 54 (1951): 286–95.

will have at least one in mixed strategies.[16] Setting the partial derivatives of E_D with respect to q and r, and of E_S with respect to s, equal to 0, and solving these equations simultaneously, one can show that when D chooses his strategy of $q = \frac{12}{13}$ and $r = 0$, which makes S indifferent between T and T̄, and S chooses $s = \frac{8}{17}$, which makes D indifferent in his choice of q (his choice of $r = 0$, whenever $s < \frac{8}{9}$, is determined by the fact that he wants to maximize E_D), means that neither player can do better, and may do worse, by choosing different values of q, r, or s.

The resulting expected payoffs for S (2.31) and D (7.53) turn out to be exactly what S and D's guarantee strategies ensure for each. That this outcome is Pareto-inferior to outcomes that other strategy pairs in table 4.1 offer the players illustrates that Nash stability and (relatively) high payoffs are not necessarily compatible in the Truth Game.

16. Nash, ''Non-cooperative Games.''

5 Conclusions

The evidence seems to me incontestable that game theory captures a substantial part of the logical basis and empirical reality of superpower conflict and provides a unified framework for its analysis. Indeed, I would go further: without modeling different aspects of this conflict as games played by rational decision makers in Washington and Moscow, one can gain only a shallow understanding of why this conflict has been so maddeningly frustrating yet persistent over the last forty years.

There are good reasons why this conflict, and the rancor and recriminations it has generated, will not simply disappear. Generally speaking, they are not rooted in inexorable historical forces, the obtuse choices of leaders, or rank misperceptions that the leaders harbor of each other. Rather, I believe, it is the unforgiving nature of the games the superpowers play that better explains their continuing conflict, though why these particular games occur and not others is less easy to answer.

I think one reason that games like Chicken and Prisoners' Dilemma are so prominent is that superpower conflict is, for the most part, not zero-sum: both sides can benefit from cooperation, at least of a limited sort. At the same time, there seems to be a kind of zero-sum competition for allies, which n-person game-theoretic coalition models of the kind Riker pioneered are useful in protraying.[1] I have not tried to analyze this broader conflict for coalition partners here, but obviously the context in which Soviet-American conflict occurs cannot be ignored, especially if its origins are to be understood.

1. William H. Riker, *The Theory of Political Coalitions* (New Haven: Yale University Press, 1962).

Whatever the origins of this conflict, its durability, I think, stems from the fact that there are no clear-cut solutions, as such, to the nonzero-sum games that seem best to model the main features of superpower conflict. Also, institutions like the United Nations, or nonaligned nations that have a manifest interest in preventing East-West conflict—and that normally might be expected to mediate the superpower conflict—have not been significant players in most of the serious clashes between the superpowers since World War II. Here again our understanding of these other forces, and how they come into play, remains inchoate.

That is why it seemed to me reasonable to restrict my focus to the two-person games played between the superpowers. Even within this restricted domain, however, it is not apparent what parts of game theory to bring to bear in modeling this seemingly intransigent conflict.

Essentially, my choices have been eclectic. Starting from classical two-person noncooperative game theory, I have tried to adapt this theory to the situations being modeled, introducing new formal concepts (for example, of power) where they seemed appropriate. Rather than next turning to simply a review of this theory and the different applications I have made of it, however, I shall stress instead the insights the models I have developed offer in (1) understanding the nature of the conflict and (2) possibly abating its severity.

I hasten to add that the prescriptions I offer are initimately tied to the theoretical perspective that game theory provides. Thus, there is nothing in what I say about preventing the ascension of pathological personalities to high office, making weapon systems less destructive, or reforming ideologies. Rather, what I propose is manipulating rules and the play of games so as to encourage more cooperative choices that lead to less vehement confrontations or that diminish the possibility of terrifying conflict.

Unless games themselves are transformed by changing their rules, I see little prospect of significant progress being made in lessening the basis of recurrent conflict between the superpowers. The problem is less that an opponent has sinister motives, or that the system he represents is evil, than the incorrigible fact that he acts belligerently because it is rational to do so.

Changing rules can alter rational choices and even transform one game into another. Thereby intractable games, however they arose, may be rendered more tractable and perhaps susceptible to cooperative solutions. The advantage that this perspective provides is that solutions are not ad hoc but grounded in the strategic character of the conflict between the superpowers and the possibility for its transformation into something more benign. Moreover, one makes no assumptions about basic changes in outlook or values—the same logic governs player choices before and after the rules change. This logic, in addition, is an ordinary one that does not presume extraordinary or heroic actions but only what it is in the interest of rational decision makers to do.

Under each of the three major topics of this book, I shall briefly discuss what the game-theoretic models reveal about the central strategic problem the players face and then possible means for ameliorating it.

5.1. Deterrence

The problem of deterrence is epitomized by the game of Chicken, although other games were used to model specific instances of crises related to deterrence (or its breakdown) that have arisen between the superpowers. Basically, the task of a player who desires to deter an adversary is to make the choice of aggression sufficiently unattractive, through the threat of retaliation if the aggression occurs, that the adversary will be deterred from initiating aggression in the first place.

The difficulty with this strategy, at least in Chicken, is that the threatener will hurt himself, as well as his adversary, if he is forced to carry out his threat, after being attacked, making the threat appear incredible. I suggested that one way a threatener could increase the credibility of his threat would be to keep his response to a provocation in doubt via a probabilistic threat. It could still be effective in the sense that, even if it were not carried out with certainty, his adversary would still suffer, on the average, from committing aggression. Also, the threatenee could never be sure that his dreaded worst outcome was foreclosed, which would be an especially telling concern if he were risk-averse.

Robust threats seem an optimal compromise between the need to be effective and credible. They always hurt the aggressor when carried out but have the additional advantage of equalizing the damage he suffers—and also the costs to the threatener in carrying out a robust threat—whatever strategy either player thinks the other will choose.

Because each side will suffer the same loss in switching from cooperation to noncooperation, whatever his opponent chooses, misperceptions will not change each side's assessments of the probable loss it will incur. Hence, it does not matter what one's opponent chooses, or one thinks it will choose: the risk associated with a robust threat is independent of its choice.

Presumably, then, robust threats lose none of their deterrent value whatever information—accurate or inaccurate—the players have of the intended actions of their opponents. This kind of invulnerability seems to me desirable and therefore should be encouraged.

In fact, both superpowers' threats today are fundamentally probabilistic because of the uncertainties, under current operational procedures, associated with responding to an attack, especially one of indeterminate magnitude and origin. However, making these threats as robust as possible has not been recognized as a conceptual solution to the dual problem of the incredibility of MAD, on the one hand, and the instability of a kind of minimal deterrence, on the other.

Probabilistic threats may have certain equivalents in the form of deterministic actions that raise the stakes of conflict but stop short of nuclear war, such as the U.S. blockade of Cuba in 1962 and the precautionary alert of U.S. military forces during the Yom Kippur War in 1973. Although these actions in the end had salutary consequences, they seem mostly to have been ad hoc responses to a worsening situation for the United States.

An understanding that probabilistic threats combine effectiveness and credibility, and that robustness can help to ensure their stability, seems to offer one resolution of the rationality crisis. Detailed practical procedures for transforming Chicken into a less menacing game through the use of robust threats, however, require much study.

Even at a theoretical level, robust strategies depend on both players' judicious use of probabilistic threats not only to render aggression unprofitable but also to elevate compromise in Chicken to a mutually best outcome in a new game in which the players' cooperative strategies are strictly dominant. Nevertheless, I think the great anguish that the apparent irrationality of deterrence has caused can perhaps be partially alleviated by an understanding that perilous games like Chicken need not be fixed in concrete but are, instead, subject to manipulation that may enable the players to avoid humiliating subjugation or even more gruesome consequences.

5.2. The Arms Race

The ongoing arms race perhaps conjures up a less apocalyptic vision than a sudden crisis that flares up and produces a major confrontation between the superpowers. Yet, its continuing burden over the past forty years not only has been an enormous economic drain but has stultified opportunities in many other areas as well. Unlike in Chicken, the problem here, as mirrored in Prisoners' Dilemma, is not that there is not an obvious rational "solution" to this game (there is—noncooperation) but that it is clearly unappealing in comparison with cooperation.

Cooperation, however, is a dominated strategy for both sides and, even if achieved, would then be an unstable outcome from which both players would have an immediate incentive to defect. Consequently, both players would seem well advised to choose their dominant non-cooperative strategies of arming: whatever the other side does, this strategy leads to a better outcome for each player.

The challenge in Prisoners' Dilemma is to change the rules to alter the dominance of the noncooperative strategy and stabilize the cooperative outcome. In fact, the cooperative outcome is a nonmyopic equilibrium, according to the theory of moves, but so also is the noncooperative outcome, which is the present status quo.

It is by no means clear how the players can be motivated to move from the latter equilibrium, given the arrant risks of acting unilaterally. Even though the cooperative outcome, once achieved, would also be stable if the players were farsighted and could move and countermove in sequential play, the problem remains of how to break out of the status quo without having one's position exploited by a treacherous act.

A more satisfactory resolution of the arms race rests, I believe, on a policy of conditional cooperation, with cooperation conditional on each side's being able to ascertain with reasonable confidence that the other side cooperated when it promised it would. I showed how reconnaissance satellites and other national technical means of verification, which each side now possesses and can utilize without dependence on the other side, can make cooperation, on an expected-value basis, rational in Prisoners' Dilemma.

Indeed, many of the limited Soviet-American agreements reached since the early 1960s seem largely a function of the increased technological capabilities of each side to monitor the military activities of the other side. Problems of monitoring remain formidable, however, especially with smaller and more mobile weapons systems (for example, cruise missiles) now easier to conceal. At the same time, such systems are less vulnerable to a first strike, vitiating the advantages of preemption.

The sharing of intelligence data, as shown by one of the models, can give the edge to a cooperative strategy insofar as it makes detection of any treaty violations increasingly probable. Thereby, each side is more likely to be deterred from attempting to cheat, which may help to "lock" the players into cooperation rather than noncooperation. Since both would prefer the former to the latter outcome in Prisoners' Dilemma, the goal becomes to identify emendations in the rules of the game that make the players' strategy choices sufficiently transparent that cheating is made counterproductive.

In a world of uncertainty, no precautions that either side takes will ever be foolproof. But this does not mean that Prisoners' Dilemma is completely refractory; in modeling the superpower arms race, a modification of the rules suggested how this conflict might be mitigated. In particular, if one conceptualizes this race as a multistage game with detection, a cooperative initiative by one or both sides can induce the rational choice of mutual cooperation when there are sufficient guarantees against being double-crossed. Even if such an initiative fails, however, it might still be a rational choice for the initiator if his monitoring capabilities alert him quickly enough to possible dangers or treaty violations, making it possible for him to recover before sustaining unacceptable losses.

The most defensible resolution of the dilemma in the arms race, I believe, is to enlarge the information pool available to the players in such a way that they can feel reasonable assurance that their cooperative choices will be detected and reciprocated. Reciprocity will be rational, in fact, if the two sides perceive as the likely alternative mutual noncooperation—unsatisfactory for both—rather than their being double-crossed. A player's trust will not be misplaced if it is undergirded by monitoring capabilities that make the success of a double-cross strategy bleak.

5.3. Verification

I have already indicated how intelligence capabilities can deter one side from lying about its adherence to an arms-control agreement and instead induce it to cooperate if it believes this cooperation will be reciprocated. However, a policy of conditional cooperation may not always be optimal for a detector if, as in the Truth Game, it is rational for the signaler to lie because the expected rewards for mendacity are greater than those for being truthful.

To elicit the truth, a more sophisticated inducement policy than straight tit-for-tat may be called for. In particular, I showed that all statements that are detected to be lies should be disbelieved, but statements that are thought to be truthful should, on occasion, also be disbelieved to offer a greater inducement for truthful behavior. This strange result held whether the detector sought to guarantee himself a certain minimum, whatever the signaler did, or he acted to induce the signaler to be truthful in an effort to do still better.

From the signaler's viewpoint, it was optimal for him *almost* always to be truthful to induce the detector to believe, regardless of what he detected. In other words, the signaler can make it advantageous for the detector to abandon a policy of conditional belief and make his belief unconditional, but this requires largely honest behavior on the part of the signaler to make this kind of unquestioning belief (or trust) rational.

I think this is a hopeful result, because it suggests that honesty "pays," at least most of the time. Of course, if a player develops a well-deserved reputation for honesty, he will be in a position, in a critical situation, to lie and probably be believed—despite contrary evidence—because of his unblemished reputation before the prevarication occurs.

One must guard scrupulously against such beguiling moments, because these are exactly the occasions when there may be good reason to suspect perfidy and *not* to doubt one's intelligence when it warns of deception.[2] On the other hand, a policy of unremitting skepticism in the

2. Richard K. Betts, *Surprise Attack: Lessons for Defense Planning* (Washington, DC: Brookings Institution, 1982); Donald C. Daniel and Katherine L. Herbig, eds., *Strategic Military Deception* (New York: Pergamon, 1982); and Klaus Knorr and Patrick Morgan, eds., *Strategic Military Surprise: Incentives and Opportunities* (New

face of positive signals may be even more deleterious to cooperation, because it undermines the basis for even trying to work out mutually rewarding agreements.

Probably the most important lesson of the signal/detection analysis is that inducement strategies may lead to higher payoffs than guarantee strategies for both the signaler and the detector. Since the superpowers assume on occasion each of these sender/receiver roles in the arms race, they would seem well advised not just to set a floor under their expected payoffs but instead to try to influence the other side—either to be mostly truthful (signaler) or to believe generally the signals it receives (detector).

These inducement strategies, as I demonstrated, are not paragons of undiluted reciprocity or untainted honesty, but they tend toward these ideals and lead to better social outcomes, on the average, than always playing it safe and taking no cooperative initiatives. To be sure, the player that takes the initiative when the other responds to it does best, so there will presumably be some jockeying to influence one's opponent rather than be influenced. But this is healthier, I believe, than adopting a dour worst-case posture that leaves little room for escaping from impasse and a thoroughly abject state of affairs.

Perhaps a larger lesson of this book is that the harrowing games I have focused on need not be candidates for utter despair. We may wish the strategic problems the superpowers face were not so obdurate, but, in a curious way, their very obduracy forces the players to come to grips with the haunting dilemmas, especially involving the use of nuclear weapons, to which these games give rise. These dilemmas may be vexing but they are not insoluble—at least one can cope with them, even if there is no magic key that resolves them. Moreover, proficient coping strategies call less for a steely cold rationality or heartless cunning and more for honesty, far-sightedness, tolerable risk-taking, and cooperation that is reciprocated.

Brunswick, NJ: Transaction, 1983). For game-theoretic and related models of deception and surprise attack, see the citations in chapter 2, n. 9, and chapter 4, n. 13, above. Michael I. Handel distinguishes diplomatic from military surprise and gives several case studies of the former in *The Diplomacy of Surprise: Hitler, Nixon, Sadat* (Cambridge, MA: Harvard University Press, 1981).

Glossary

This glossary contains definitions of game-theoretic and related terms used in this book. An attempt has been made to define these terms in relatively nontechnical language; more extended and rigorous definitions of some concepts (for example, the three different kinds of power) can be found in the text.

Backward induction. Backward induction is a reasoning process in which players, working backward from the bottom to the top of a game tree, anticipate each other's rational choices.

Certain equivalent. A certain equivalent is a deterministic action whose value is the same as the expected value of a probabilistic action (for example, a threat).

Choice rule. In a two-person game, a choice rule is a conditional strategy based on one player's prediction of the strategy choice of the other.

Complete information. A game is one of complete information if the players know each others' preferences or payoffs for every outcome and the rules of play.

Conditional cooperation. In a two-person game, conditional cooperation is a choice rule that says that a player will cooperate if he predicts the other player will cooperate; otherwise he will not.

Conditional probability. A conditional probability is a probability that is dependent on the occurrence of a prior event.

Constant-sum (zero-sum) game. A constant-sum game is a game in which the payoffs to the players at every outcome sum to come constant (or zero); all constant-sum games can be converted into zero-sum games by subtracting the appropriate constant from the payoffs to the players.

Credibility of a threat. *See* Incredibility of a threat.

Credible threat. A credible threat is a probabilistic threat that is just sufficient to deter a threatenee.

Deception strategy. In a game of incomplete information, a deception strategy is a player's false announcement of his preferences to induce the other player to choose a strategy favorable to the deceiver.

Deterrence. Deterrence is a policy of threatening retaliation against noncooperation by an opponent to deter him from choosing non-cooperation in the first place.

Dominant strategy. A dominant strategy is a strategy that leads to outcomes at least as good as those of any other strategy for all possible choices of other players and to a better outcome for at least one set of choices.

Dominated strategy. A dominated strategy is a strategy that leads to outcomes no better than those given by any other strategy for all possible choices of other players and to a worse outcome for at least one set of choices.

Effectiveness of a threat. The effectiveness of a threat is the loss in expected payoff the threatenee suffers when the threatener carries out his threat.

Effective power. In a two-person game, a player's power is effective if he is able to induce a different (and usually better) outcome for himself when he possesses this power than when the other player possesses it.

Effective threat. An effective threat is a deterministic threat that is always carried out.

Expected payoff. An expected payoff is the sum of the payoffs a player receives from each outcome multiplied by its probability of occurrence, for all possible outcomes that may arise.

Extensive form. A game in extensive form is represented by a game tree in which players are assumed to make sequential choices.

Final outcome. In a sequential game, the final outcome is the outcome induced by (possible) rational moves and countermoves from the initial outcome according to the theory of moves.

Game. A game is the sum total of the rules of play that describe it.

Game of partial conflict. A game of partial confict is a variable-sum game in which the players' preferences are not diametrically opposed.

Game of total conflict. A game of total conflict is a constant-sum game in which what one player gains the other players lose.

Game theory. Game theory is a mathematical theory of strategy to explicate optimal choices in interdependent decision situations, wherein the outcome depends on the choices of two or more actors or players.

Game tree. A game tree is a symbolic tree based on the rules of play of the game, in which the vertices, or nodes, of the tree represent choice points and the branches represent alternative courses of action that can be chosen.

Guarantee strategy. A guarantee strategy is a strategy that ensures a player of a particular minimum expected payoff, independent of the strategy choices of the other players.

Incredibility of a threat. The incredibility of a threat is the loss in expected payoff the threatener suffers when he carries out his threat.

Inducement strategy. An inducement strategy is one in which an inducer offers an incentive to an inducee to choose a particular strategy, in order to maximize his (the inducee's) expected payoff, that also favors the inducer.

Information set. An information set is the set of vertices, or nodes, on a game tree that are indistinguishable to the players.

Initial outcome. In a sequential game, the initial outcome is the outcome rational players choose when they make their initial strategy choices according to the theory of moves.

Isoline. An isoline defines a boundary at which a player's expected payoff is constant.

Lexicographic decision rule. A lexicographic decision rule enables a player to rank outcomes on the basis of a most important criterion (''primary goal''), then a next most important criterion (''secondary goal''), and so forth.

Metagame theory. Metagame theory is a theory about games in which players choose strategies with knowledge or expectations about the choices of other players.

Minimal deterrence. Minimal deterrence occurs when a threat is credible.

Minimax strategy. *See* Guarantee strategy.

Mixed strategy. In a normal-form game, a mixed strategy is a strategy that involves the random selection from two or more pure strategies, according to a particular probability distribution.

Moving power. In a two-person sequential game, moving power is the ability to continue moving when the other player must eventually stop.

Mutual assured destruction (MAD). Mutual assured destruction (or deterrence) is a policy of always retaliating against aggression by the other player, which implies a deterministic threat of responding with certainty to noncooperation with a strategy of non-cooperation oneself.

Nash equilibrium. In a normal-form game, a Nash equilibrium is an outcome from which no player would have an incentive to depart unilaterally because he would do (immediately) worse, or at least not better, if he moved.

Node. A node is a point in a game tree at which a player (or chance) makes choices.

No first use. No first use is a policy of never being the first to use nuclear weapons, which precludes being the first to choose non-cooperation in a game modelling nuclear deterrence.

Nonmyopic calculation. In a two-person sequential game, non-myopic calculation is based on the assumption that rational players make choices in full anticipation of how each will respond to the other, both in selecting their strategies initially and making subsequent moves.

Nonmyopic equilibrium. In a two-person sequential game, a non-myopic equilibrium is an outcome from which neither player, anticipating all possible rational moves and countermoves from the initial outcome, would have an incentive to depart because he would do (eventually) worse, or at least not better, if he did.

Normal form. A game in normal form is represented by an outcome/payoff matrix in which players are assumed to choose their strategies independently.

Ordinal game. An ordinal game is a game in which the players can rank, but not necessarily assign payoffs or utilities, to the outcomes.

Outcome/payoff matrix. In a game in normal form, an outcome/payoff matrix is a rectangular array, or matrix, whose entries indicate the outcomes/payoffs to each player resulting from each of their possible strategy choices.

Pareto-inferior/superior outcome. An outcome is Pareto-inferior if there exists another outcome that is better for some players and not worse for all the other players. If there is no such other outcome, the outcome in question is Pareto-superior.

Payoff. A payoff is the utility, or numerical value, that a player attaches to an outcome in a game.

Perfect equilibrium. A perfect equilibrium is an outcome that, when threatened, is rational for the threatener to implement in an extensive-form game.

Perfect information. A game is one of perfect information if each player knows with certainty the strategy choice or move of every other player at each point in the sequence of play.

Preemption. Preemption is a player's choice of noncooperation in a game before his opponent makes this choice.

Preference. The preference of a player is his ranking of outcomes from best to worst.

Probabilistic threat. A probabilistic threat is a threat that is carried out with a probability less than one.

Pure strategy. In a game in normal form, a pure strategy is a single strategy chosen with certainty.

Rational player. A rational player is one who seeks to attain better outcomes, according to his preference, in light of the presumed rational choices of other players in a game.

Robust threats (deterrent strategies). Robust threats ensure that each player will suffer the same loss in switching from cooperation to noncooperation, whatever strategy his opponent chooses.

Rules of play. The rules of play of a game describe the preferences and choices available to the players, their sequencing, and any special prerogatives (for example, power) one player may have in the play of the game.

Security level. In a normal-form game, the security level of a player is the best outcome or payoff he can ensure for himself, whatever strategies the other players choose.

Sequential game. A sequential game is one in which players can move and countermove after their initial strategy choices according to the theory of moves.

Staying power. In a two-person sequential game, staying power is the ability of a player to hold off making a strategy choice until the other player has made his.

Strategy. In a game in normal form, a strategy is a complete plan that specifies all possible courses of action of a player for whatever contingencies may arise.

Supergame. A supergame is a game that comprises repeated plays of a nonsequential game.

Symmetric game. A symmetrical game is a two-person game in which the ranks of the outcomes by the players along the main diagonal are the same, whereas the ranks of the off-diagonal outcomes are mirror images of each other.

Theory of moves. The theory of moves describes optimal strategic calculations in normal-form games in which the players can move and countermove from an initial outcome in sequential play.

Threat power. In a two-person sequential game that is repeated, threat power is the ability of a player to threaten a mutually disadvantageous outcome in the single play of a game to deter untoward actions in the future play of this or other games.

Tit-for-tat. *See* Conditional cooperation.

Undominated strategy. An undominated strategy is a strategy that is neither unconditionally best, or dominant, nor unconditionally worst, or dominated.

Variable-sum game. A variable-sum game is a game in which the sum of the payoffs to the players at different outcomes varies, so the players may gain or lose simultaneously at different outcomes.

Verification. Verification involves determining the correspondence between the statements and the observed actions of an opponent.

Zero-sum game. *See* Constant-sum (zero-sum) game.

Bibliography

Abel, Elie. *The Missile Crisis.* Philadelphia: Lippincott, 1966.

Allen, Thomas B., and Norman Polmar. "The Silent Chase: Tracking Soviet Submarines." *New York Times Magazine,* January 1, 1984, pp. 13–17, 26–27.

Allison, Graham T. *Essence of Decision: Explaining the Cuban Missile Crisis.* Boston: Little, Brown, 1971.

Aspin, Les. "The Verification of the SALT II Agreement." *Scientific American* 240, no. 2 (February 1979): 38–45.

Axelrod, R. "Coping with Deception." In *Applied Game Theory: Proceedings of a Conference at the Institute for Advanced Studies, Vienna, June 13–16, 1978,* ed. S. J. Brams, A. Schotter, and G. Schwödiauer, pp. 390–405. Würzburg, West Germany: Physica-Verlag, 1979.

Axelrod, Robert. *The Evolution of Cooperation.* New York: Basic, 1984.

Axelrod, Robert. "The Rational Timing of Surprise." *World Politics* 31, no. 2 (January 1979):228–46.

Baugh, William H. *The Politics of Nuclear Balance: Ambiguity and Continuity in Strategic Policies.* New York: Longman, 1984.

Bethe, Hans A., Richard L. Garwin, and Henry W. Kendall. "Spaced-Based Ballistic Missile Defense." *Scientific American* 251, no. 4 (October 1984): 37–47.

Betts, Richard K. *Surprise Attack: Lessons for Defense Planning.* Washington, DC: Brookings Institution, 1982.

Biddle, W. F. *Weapons, Technology, and Arms Control.* New York: Praeger, 1972.

Blechman, Barry M., and Douglas M. Hart. "The Political Utility of Nuclear Weapons: The 1973 Middle East Crisis." *International Security* 7, no. 1 (Summer 1982):132–56.

Blechman, Barry M., and Stephen S. Kaplan. *Force without War: U.S. Armed Forces as a Political Instrument.* Washington, DC: Brookings Institution, 1978.

Bok, Sissela. *Lying: Moral Choice in Public and Private Life.* New York: Pantheon, 1978.

Boulding, Kenneth E., ed. *Peace and the War Industry.* New Brunswick, NJ: Transaction, 1973.

Bova, Ben. *Assured Survival: Putting the Star Wars Defense in Perspective.* Boston: Houghton Mifflin, 1984.

Bracken, Paul. *The Command and Control of Nuclear Forces.* New Haven: Yale University Press, 1984.

Brams, Steven J. "Deception in 2 × 2 Games." *Journal of Peace Science* 2 (Spring 1977):171–203.

Brams, Steven J. *Game Theory and Politics.* New York: Free Press, 1975.

Brams, Steven J. "Newcomb's Problem and Prisoners' Dilemma." *Journal of Conflict Resolution* 19, no. 4 (December 1975):596–612.

Brams, Steven J. "Omniscience and Omnipotence: How They May Help—or Hurt—in a Game." *Inquiry* 25, no. 2 (June 1982):217–31.

Brams, Steven J. *Paradoxes in Politics: An Introduction to the Nonobvious in Political Science.* New York: Free Press, 1976.

Brams, Steven J. *Superior Beings: If They Exist, How Would We Know? Game-Theoretic Implications of Omniscience, Omnipotence, Immortality, and Incomprehensibility.* New York: Springer-Verlag, 1983.

Brams, Steven J., and Morton D. Davis. "The Verification Problem in Arms Control: A Game-Theoretic Analysis." Economic Research Report no. 83–12, C. V. Starr Center for Applied Economics, New York University, October 1983.

Brams, Steven J., Morton D. Davis, and Philip D. Straffin, Jr. "Comment on Wagner, 'The Theory of Games and the Problem of International Cooperation.'" *American Political Science Review* 78, no. 2 (June 1984):495.

Brams, Steven J., Morton D. Davis, and Philip D. Straffin, Jr. "The Geometry of the Arms Race." *International Studies Quarterly* 23, no. 4 (December 1979):567–88.

Brams, Steven J., Morton D. Davis, and Philip D. Straffin, Jr. "A Reply to 'Detection and Disarmament.'" *International Studies Quarterly* 23, no. 4 (December 1979):599–600.

Brams, Steven J., and Marek P. Hessel. "Absorbing Outcomes in 2 × 2 Games." *Behavioral Science* 27, no. 4 (October 1982):393–401.

Brams, Steven J., and Marek P. Hessel. "Staying Power in 2 × 2 Games." *Theory and Decision* 15, no. 3 (September 1983):279–302.

Brams, Steven J., and Marek P. Hessel. "Threat Power in Sequential Games." *International Studies Quarterly* 28, no. 1 (March 1984):15–36.

Brams, Steven J., and D. Marc Kilgour. "Optimal Deterrence." Department of Politics, New York University. 1984. Mimeographed.

Brams, Steven J., and Donald Wittman. "Nonmyopic Equilibria in 2 × 2 Games." *Conflict Management and Peace Science* 6, no. 1 (Fall 1981):39–62.

Brams, Steven J., and Frank C. Zagare. "Deception in Simple Voting Games." *Social Science Research* 6 (September 1977):257–72.

Brams, Steven J., and Frank C. Zagare. "Double Deception: Two against One in Three-Person Games." *Theory and Decision* 13, no. 1 (March 1981):81–90.

Brown, Harold. *Thinking about National Security: Defense and Foreign Policy in a Dangerous World*. Boulder, CO: Westview, 1983.

Buchheim, Robert W., and Dan Caldwell. "The US-USSR Standing Consultative Commission: Description and Appraisal." Center for Foreign Policy Development, Brown University. 1983. Mimeographed.

Bueno de Mesquita, Bruce. *The War Trap*. New Haven: Yale University Press, 1981.

Bundy, McGeorge. "The Bishops and the Bomb." *New York Review of Books,* June 16, 1983, pp. 3–8.

Bundy, McGeorge S., George F. Kennan, Robert S. McNamara, and Gerard Smith. "Nuclear Weapons and the Atlantic Alliance." *Foreign Affairs* 60 (Spring 1982):753–68.

Bunn, Matthew, and Kosta Tsipis. "The Uncertainties of a Preemptive Nuclear Attack." *Scientific American* 249, no. 5 (November 1983):38–47.

Chayes, Abram. *The Cuban Missile Crisis: International Crises and the Role of Law.* New York: Oxford University Press, 1974.

Cioffi-Revilla, Claudio. "A Probability Model of Credibility." *Journal of Conflict Resolution* 27, no. 1 (March 1983):73–108.

Cox, Arthur Macy. *Russian Roulette—The Superpower Game.* New York: Times Books, 1982.

Dacey, Raymond, "Detection and Disarmament: A Comment on 'The Geometry of the Arms Race.' " *International Studies Quarterly* 23, no. 4 (December 1979):589–98.

Dacey, Raymond. "Detection, Inference and the Arms Race." In *Reason and Decision,* Bowling Green Studies in Applied Philosophy, vol. III—1981, ed. Michael Bradie and Kenneth Sayre, pp. 87–100. Bowling Green, OH: Applied Philosophy Program, Bowling Green State University, 1982.

Daniel, Donald C., and Katherine L. Herbig, eds. *Strategic Military Deception.* New York: Pergamon, 1982.

Davis, Morton D. *Game Theory: A Nontechnical Introduction,* rev. ed. New York: Basic, 1983.

Detzer, David. *The Brink: Story of the Cuban Missile Crisis.* New York: Crowell, 1979.

Dinerstein, Herbert. *The Making of the Cuban Missile Crisis, October 1962.* Baltimore: Johns Hopkins University Press, 1976.

Divine, Robert A., ed. *The Cuban Missile Crisis.* Chicago: Quadrangle, 1971.

Draper, Theodore. *Present History.* New York: Random House, 1983.

Dyson, Freeman, *Weapons and Hope.* New York: Harper and Row, 1984.

Ellsberg, Daniel. "The Theory and Practice of Blackmail." In *Bargaining: Formal Theories of Negotiation,* ed. Oran R. Young, pp. 343–63. Urbana, IL: University of Illinois Press, 1975.

Elster, Jon. *Ulysses and the Sirens: Studies in Rationality and Irrationality.* Cambridge: Cambridge University Press, 1979.

Epstein, William. "The Role of the Public in the Decisionmaking Process for Arms Limitation." In *Decisionmaking for Arms Limitation: Assessments and Prospects,* ed. Hans Guenter Brauch and Duncan L. Clarke, pp. 277–93. Cambridge, MA: Ballinger, 1983.

Fischer, Dietrich. *Preventing War in the Nuclear Age.* Totowa, NJ: Rowman and Allanheld, 1984.

Fishburn, Peter C. "Lexicographic Orders, Utilities and Decision Rules: A Survey." *Management Science* 20 (July 1974):1442–71.

Fraser, Niall M., and Keith W. Hipel. "Dynamic Modeling of the Cuban Missile Crisis." *Conflict Management and Peace Science* 6, no. 2 (Spring 1982–83):1–18.

Freedman, Lawrence. *The Evolution of Nuclear Strategy.* New York: St. Martin's, 1981.

Frye, Alton. "Strategic Restraint: Mutual and Assured." *Foreign Policy* 27 (Summer 1977):3–24.

Gamson, William A., and André Modigliani. *Untangling the Cold War: A Strategy for Testing Rival Theories.* Boston: Little, Brown, 1971.

Garthoff, Raymond L. "The Role of Nuclear Weapons: Soviet Perceptions." In *Nuclear Negotiations: Reassessing Arms Control Goals in U.S.-Soviet Relations,* ed. Alan F. Neidle, pp. 10–13. Austin, TX: Lyndon B. Johnson School of Public Affairs, 1982.

Gauthier, David. "Deterrence, Maximization, and Rationality." *Ethics* 94, no. 3 (April 1984):474–95.

George, Alexander, L., and Richard Smoke. *Deterrence in American Foreign Policy: Theory and Practice.* New York: Columbia University Press, 1974.

George, Alexander L., et al. *Managing U.S.-Soviet Rivalry: Problems of Crisis Prevention.* Boulder, CO: Westview, 1983.

Gillespie, John V., et al. "An Optimal Control Model of Arms Races." *American Political Science Review* 71, no. 1 (March 1977):226–44.

Glassman, Jon D. *Arms for the Arabs: The Soviet Union and War in the Middle East.* Baltimore: Johns Hopkins University Press, 1975.

Gottfried, Kurt, Henry W. Kendall, and John M. Lee. " 'No First Use' of Nuclear Weapons." *Scientific American* 250, no. 3 (March 1984):33–41.

Gray, Colin S. *Strategic Studies and Public Policy.* Lexington, KY: University Press of Kentucky, 1982.

Greenwood, Ted. "Reconnaissance and Arms Control." *Scientific American* 228, no. 2 (February 1973):14–25.

Gwertzman, Bernard. "Reagan Is Said to Find Breaches by Soviets of Agreements on Arms." *New York Times,* January 24, 1984, p. 1.

Handel, Michael I. *The Diplomacy of Surprise: Hitler, Nixon, Sadat.* Cambridge, MA: Harvard University Press, 1981.

Hardin, Russell. "Unilateral Versus Mutual Disarmament." *Philosophy & Public Affairs* 12, no. 3 (April 1983):236–54.

Harvard Nuclear Study Group. *Living with Nuclear Weapons.* New York: Bantam, 1983.

Henderson, John M., and Richard E. Quandt. *Microeconomic Theory: A Mathematical Approach,* 2d ed. New York: McGraw-Hill, 1971.

Hirshleifer, Jack. "The Economic Approach to Conflict." Department of Economics, University of California, Los Angeles. 1984. Mimeographed.

Holloway, David. *The Soviet Union and the Arms Race.* New Haven: Yale University Press, 1983.

Holst, Johan J. "What Is Really Going On?" *Foreign Policy* 19 (Summer 1975):155–63.

Holsti, Ole R., Richard A. Brody, and Robert C. North. "Measuring Affect and Action in International Reaction Models: Empirical Materials from the 1962 Cuban Crisis." *Journal of Peace Research* 1 (1964):170–89.

Howard, Michael. *The Causes of War and Other Essays.* Cambridge, MA: Harvard University Press, 1983.

Howard, Nigel. *Paradoxes of Rationality: Theory of Metagames and Political Behavior.* Cambridge, MA: MIT Press, 1971.

Intriligator, Michael D., and Dagobert L. Brito. "Can Arms Races Lead to the Outbreak of War?" *Journal of Conflict Resolution* 28, no. 1 (March 1984):63–84.

Intriligator, Michael D., and Dagobert L. Brito. "Formal Models of Arms Races." *Journal of Peace Science* 2 (Spring 1977):77–96.

Jervis, Robert. *The Illogic of American Nuclear Strategy.* Ithaca, NY: Cornell University Press, 1984.

Kahn, Herman. *On Escalation: Metaphors and Scenarios.* New York: Praeger, 1965.

Kaplan, Fred. *The Wizards of Armageddon.* New York: Simon and Schuster, 1983.

Kilgour, D. Marc. "Anticipation and Stability in Two-Person Non-Cooperative Games." Department of Mathematics, Wilfred Laurier University [Canada]. 1984. Mimeographed.

Kilgour, D. Marc. "Equilibria for Far-sighted Players." *Theory and Decision* 16, no. 2 (March 1984):135–57.

Knorr, Klaus, and Patrick Morgan, eds. *Strategic Military Surprise: Incentives and Opportunities.* New Brunswick, NJ: Transaction, 1983.

Krauthammer, Charles. "On Nuclear Morality." In *Nuclear Arms: Ethics, Strategy, Politics,* ed. R. James Woolsey, pp. 11–21. San Francisco: Institute for Contemporary Studies, 1984.

Leontief, Wassily W.,and Faye Duchin. *Military Spending: Facts and Figures, Worldwide Implications, and Future Outlook.* New York: Oxford University Press, 1983.

Lodal, Jan M. "Verifying SALT." *Foreign Policy* 24 (Fall 1976):40–64.

Long, Frederick A. "Arms Control from the Perspective of the Nineteen-Seventies." In *Arms, Defense Policy, and Arms Control,* ed. Frederick A. Long et al., pp. 1–13. New York: Norton, 1975.

Luce, Duncan, and Howard Raiffa. *Games and Decisions: Introduction and Critical Survey.* New York: Wiley, 1957.

Luterbacher, Urs. "Last Words About War?" *Journal of Conflict Resolution* 28, no. 1 (March 1984):165–81.

McGuire, Martin. *Secrecy and the Arms Race: A Theory of the Accumulation of Strategic Weapons and How Secrecy Affects It.* Cambridge, MA: Harvard University Press, 1965.

McNamara, Robert S. "Inviting War." *New York Times,* September 9, 1983, p. A27.

Majeski, Stephen J. "Arms Races as Iterated Prisoner's Dilemmas." *Mathematical Social Sciences* (forthcoming).

Maoz, Zeev. "Resolve, Capabilities, and the Outcomes of Interstate Disputes, 1816–1976." *Journal of Conflict Resolution* 27, no. 2 (June 1983):195–229.

Mearsheimer, John J. *Conventional Deterrence.* Ithaca, NY: Cornell University Press, 1983.

Meyer, Stephen M. "Verification and Risk in Arms Control." *International Security* 8, no. 4 (Spring 1984):111–26.

Morgan, Patrick M. *Deterrence: A Conceptual Analysis,* 2d ed. Beverly Hills, CA: Sage, 1983.

Muzzio, Douglas. *Watergate Games.* New York: New York University Press, 1982.

Myrdal, Alva. *The Game of Disarmament: How the United States and Russia Run the Arms Race.* New York: Random House, 1976.

Myrdal, Alva. "The International Control of Disarmament." *Scientific American* 231, no. 4 (October 1974):21–33.

Nacht, Michael L. "The Delicate Balance of Error." *Foreign Policy* 19 (Summer 1975):163–67.

Nash, John. "Non-cooperative Games." *Annals of Mathematics* 54 (1951):286–95.

Newhouse, John. *Cold Dawn: The Story of Salt.* New York: Holt, Rinehart and Winston, 1973.

Nincic, Miroslav. *The Arms Race: The Political Economy of Military Growth.* New York: Praeger, 1982.

Nixon, Richard M. *RN: The Memoirs of Richard Nixon.* New York: Grosset and Dunlap, 1978.

Owen, Guillermo. *Game Theory,* 2d ed. New York: Academic, 1982.

Pachter, Henry M. *Collision Course: The Cuban Missile Crisis and Coexistence.* New York: Praeger, 1963.

Payne, James L. *The American Threat: National Security and Foreign Policy.* College Station, TX: Lytton, 1981.

Payne, Keith B. *Nuclear Deterrence in U.S.-Soviet Relations.* Boulder, CO: Westview, 1982.

Potter, William C., ed. *Verification and SALT: The Challenge of Strategic Deception.* Boulder, CO: Westview, 1980.

Pringle, Peter, and William Arkin. *SIOP: The Secret U.S. Plan for Nuclear War.* New York: Norton, 1983.

Pursell, Carroll W., Jr., ed. *The Military-Industrial Complex.* New York: Harper and Row, 1972.

Rapoport, Anatol, and Albert Chammah. *Prisoners' Dilemma: A Study in Conflict and Cooperation.* Ann Arbor, MI: University of Michigan Press, 1965.

Rapoport, Anatol, and Melvin Guyer. "A Taxonomy of 2 × 2 Games." *General Systems: Yearbook of the Society for General Systems Research* 11 (1965):203–14.

Reese, William. "Deception in a Game Theoretic Framework." In *Strategic Military Deception,* ed. Donald C. Daniel and Katherine L. Herbig, pp. 115–35. New York: Pergamon, 1982.

Richardson, Lewis F. *Arms and Insecurity: A Mathematical Study of the Causes and Origins of War.* Pittsburgh: Boxwood, 1960.

Richelson, Jeffrey T. "The Keyhole Satellite Program." *Journal of Strategic Studies* 7, no. 2 (June 1984):212–53.

Riker, William H. *The Theory of Political Coalitions.* New Haven: Yale University Press, 1962.

Rosen, Steven, ed. *Testing the Theories of the Military-Industrial Complex*. Lexington, MA: Heath, 1973.

Russell, Clifford S. "Monitoring Sources of Pollution: Lessons from Single and Multiple Play Games." Discussion Paper 121, Quality of the Environment Division. Washington, DC: Resources for the Future, May 1984.

Russett, Bruce M. *The Prisoners of Insecurity*. San Francisco: Freeman, 1983.

Sarkesian, Sam C., ed. *The Military-Industrial Complex: A Reassessment*. Beverly Hills, CA: Sage, 1972.

Schell, Jonathan. *The Abolition*. New York: Knopf, 1984.

Schelling, Thomas C. *Arms and Influence*. New Haven: Yale University Press, 1966.

Schelling, Thomas C. *The Strategy of Conflict*. Cambridge, MA: Harvard University Press, 1960.

Scoville, Herbert, Jr. "Is Espionage Necessary for Our Society?" *Foreign Affairs* 54 (April 1976):482–95.

Shubik, Martin. *Game Theory in the Social Sciences: Concepts and Solutions*. Cambridge, MA: MIT Press, 1982.

Snow, Donald M. *The Nuclear Future: Toward a Strategy of Uncertainty*. University, AL: University of Alabama Press, 1983.

Snyder, Glenn H., and Paul Diesing. *Conflict among Nations: Bargaining, Decision Making, and Systems Structure in International Crises*. Princeton, NJ: Princeton University Press, 1977.

Sorensen, Theodore C. *Kennedy*. New York: Harper and Row, 1965.

Spanier, John W., and Joseph L. Nogee. *The Politics of Disarmament: A Study in Soviet-American Gamesmanship*. New York: Praeger, 1962.

Steinberg, Gerald M. *Satellite Reconnaissance: The Role of Informal Bargaining*. New York: Praeger, 1983.

Steinbrunner, John D., and Leon V. Sigal, eds. *Alliance Security: NATO and the No-First-Use Question*. Washington, DC: Brookings Institution, 1983.

Stockholm International Peace Research Institute. *Strategic Disarmament, Verification, and National Security*. New York: Crane, Russak, 1977.

Sykes, Lynn R., and Jack Evernden. "The Verification of a Comprehensive Nuclear Test Ban." *Scientific American* 236, no. 4 (October 1982):47–55.

Taylor, Michael. *Anarchy and Cooperation.* London: Wiley Ltd, 1976.

Tierney, John. "The Invisible Force." *Science 83* 4, no. 6 (November 1983):68–78.

Udis, Bernard, ed. *The Economic Consequences of Reduced Military Spending.* Lexington, MA: Heath, 1973.

U.S. Arms Control and Disarmament Agency. "Verification: The Critical Element in Arms Control." Washington, DC: U.S. Arms Control and Disarmament Agency, 1976.

von Neumann, John, and Oskar Morgenstern. *Theory of Games and Economic Behavior,* 3d ed. Princeton, NJ: Princeton University Press, 1953.

Wagner, R. Harrison. "The Theory of Games and the Problem of Internation Cooperation." *American Political Science Review* 77, no. 2 (June 1983):330–46.

Ward, Michael Don. "Differential Paths to Parity: A Study of the Contemporary Arms Race." *American Political Science Review* 78, no. 2 (June 1984):297–317.

Weede, Erich. "Some (Western) Dilemmas in Managing Extended Deterrence." Forschunginstitut für Soziologie, University of Cologne. 1984. Mimeographed.

Wicker, Tom. "Cheating on SALT." *New York Times,* May 3, 1983, p. A27.

Wieseltier, Leon. *Nuclear War, Nuclear Peace.* New York: Holt, Rinehart and Winston, 1983.

Wohlstetter, Albert. "The Delicate Balance of Terror." *Foreign Affairs* 37 (January 1959):209–34.

Wohlstetter, Albert. "Is There a Strategic Arms Race?" *Foreign Policy* 15 (Summer 1974):3–20 and 16 (Fall 1974):48–81.

Wohlstetter, Albert. "Optimal Ways to Confuse Ourselves." *Foreign Policy* 20 (Fall 1975):170–98.

York, Herbert F., and G. Allen Greb. "Strategic Reconnaissance." *Bulletin of Atomic Scientists* (April 1977):33–42.

Zagare, Frank C. "A Game-Theoretic Evaluation of the Cease-Fire Alert Decision of 1973." *Journal of Peace Research* 20, no. 1 (1983):73–86.

Zagare, Frank C. "Limited Move Equilibria in 2 × 2 Games." *Theory and Decision* 16, no. 1 (January 1984):1–19.

Zagare, Frank C. "The Geneva Conference of 1954: A Case of Tacit

Deception.'' *International Studies Quarterly* 23, no. 3 (September 1979):390–411.

Zagare, Frank C. ''Nonmyopic Equilibria and the Middle East Crisis of 1967.'' *Conflict Management and Peace Science* 5 (Spring 1981):139–62.

Zagare, Frank C. ''Toward a Reconciliation of Game Theory and the Theory of Mutual Deterrence.'' Department of Political Science, Boston University. 1983. Mimeographed.

Zinnes, Dina A., and John V. Gillespie, eds. *Mathematical Models in International Relations.* New York: Praeger, 1976.

Zraket, Charles A. ''Strategic Command, Control, Communications, and Intelligence.'' *Science* 224 (22 June 1984):1306–11.

Zuckerman, Solly. *Nuclear Illusion and Reality.* New York: Viking, 1982.

Index